Christopher Wordsworth

The Inspiration of the Bible

Five lectures delivered in Westminster Abbey

Christopher Wordsworth

The Inspiration of the Bible
Five lectures delivered in Westminster Abbey

ISBN/EAN: 9783337097196

Printed in Europe, USA, Canada, Australia, Japan

Cover: Foto ©Lupo / pixelio.de

More available books at **www.hansebooks.com**

THE INSPIRATION

OF THE

BIBLE:

FIVE LECTURES,

DELIVERED IN WESTMINSTER ABBEY.

BY

CHR. WORDSWORTH, D.D.

CANON OF WESTMINSTER,
VICAR OF STANFORD IN THE VALE.

LONDON:
RIVINGTONS, WATERLOO PLACE.
1861.

"In the name of HOLY SCRIPTURE we do understand those Canonical Books of the Old and New Testament, of whose authority was never any doubt in the Church."

"All the Books of the NEW TESTAMENT, as they are commonly received, we do receive and account them Canonical."

From the Sixth of the Thirty-nine Articles of the United Church of England and Ireland.

The following Lectures, on the INSPIRATION of the BIBLE, were delivered at Westminster in the months of February and March of the present year. They are entitled *Lectures* rather than *Sermons*, as being more of a theological and historical than of an expository or hortatory character: and in preparing them the Author has endeavoured to discharge, in some degree, the duty of an office assigned to him by the kindness of the Dean and Chapter of Westminster; that of Theological Lecturer in the Abbey Church.

If health and strength are given him, he purposes, with the divine help, to deliver a similar course of Lectures, " On the INTERPRETATION of the BIBLE."

Cloisters, Westminster,
Monday before Easter, 1861.

LECTURE I.[1]

1 Peter iii. 15.

Be ready always to give an answer to every man that asketh you a reason of the hope that is in you.

I. 1. The hope that is in us as Christians rests upon the belief that the Bible is the Word of God. The works of the natural Creation declare His Power, but they do not reveal to us the Mysteries of Faith. Human Reason could never have assured us that sinners may obtain pardon through God's mercy in a Redeemer, and that we may acquire spiritual grace, enabling us to do His Will. We could never have discovered by our intellectual faculties, that there is a Judgment to come, and a Resurrection of the Body, and joys eternal in heaven for those who believe and obey Him.

These are supernatural truths, and they are revealed to us in the Bible, and in the Bible alone. And by faith in these truths we are excited to do our duty to God, our neighbour, and ourselves: we are

[1] Preached in Westminster Abbey, at the Evening Service, Feb. 24.

encouraged to suffer patiently, and *to live soberly, righteously, and godly in this present world, looking for that blessed hope, and the glorious appearing of the great God and our Saviour Jesus Christ*[2]. Therefore the Apostle St. Paul says, *Whatsoever things were written aforetime were written for our learning, that we through patience and comfort of the Scriptures might have hope*[3].

2. Our spiritual Enemy knows, that belief in the Inspiration of the Bible is the foundation of Christian Faith and of Christian Virtue; and that, if "the belief in the authority of Scripture is shaken, then Christian Faith will falter, and if Christian Faith falters, then Christian Charity will fail[4]," and that the fabric of human society will be dissolved, and that men and nations will become victims of his power.

The Evil One has therefore been indefatigable in his attempts to shake this foundation. In ancient days he enlisted Kings against the Bible. He incited Antiochus Epiphanes to take up arms against the Old Testament. He raised up the Emperor Diocletian against the New. He engaged sceptical philosophers, such as Celsus, Porphyry, and Julian, in an intellectual campaign against the Word of God. He beguiled some, who called themselves

---

[2] Titus ii. 12, 13.   [3] Rom. xv. 4.
[4] S. Augustine de Doct. Christianâ i. 41, "Titubabit fides, si divinarum Scripturarum vacillat auctoritas; porrò, Fide titubante, Charitas et etiam ipsa languescit." And so Hooker (III. viii. 13) says, "The main principle whereupon our belief of all things therein contained dependeth, is that the Scriptures are the Oracles of God."

Christians, to impugn the Bible. The Marcionites and the Manichæans alleged that the Old Testament is contrary to the New. Other heretical Teachers rejected portions of both Testaments, others distorted their meaning by novel interpretations, and substituted their own imaginations in the place of the Word of God.

The Church of God, with the Bible in her hands, regards the past with thankfulness, and looks forward to the future with hope. She knows that the Holy Scriptures have already passed through a severe ordeal; and she is sure, that their Divine Author, Who has never failed to protect them, will defend them unto the end. She is persuaded, that all attacks upon the Bible will issue in its victory, and will manifest more clearly that it is the Word of God.

As the end of the world approaches, the Bible may expect new conflicts, and may hope for new conquests. Its own prophecies will be fulfilled. The Enemy of Holy Scripture will rage more fiercely, in proportion as his doom is nearer. He will make more desperate assaults upon Holy Writ, knowing that *he hath but a short time*[5].

3. The present age bears witness to this truth. England has hitherto stood high among the Nations of Europe and the World, during some centuries, for her reverent esteem of the Bible. But now a

---

[5] Rev. xii. 12.

change seems to be taking place. Persons eminent among us for high position in our Schools of Learning, and exercising great influence, by their reputation for intellectual gifts, have not hesitated to avow an opinion, that certain portions of Holy Scripture were not written by those whose names they bear, and that sundry parts of it are blemished by error, and that the Bible is not to be regarded as distinct from other Volumes, but is to be treated as a common book [6].

4. Such affirmations as these require us to examine the grounds of our own belief in the Inspiration of Holy Writ. And since it is our duty to promote the temporal and eternal happiness of others, as well as our own, we ought to be prepared to give an *answer to every one who asks us a reason of the hope that is in us.*

This then is the question to which our attention is invited;

By what reasons are we persuaded, and by what arguments would we seek to convince others, that the Bible, the whole Bible, and nothing but the Bible, is the written Word of God?

May the Holy Spirit enlighten the eyes of our understandings, and enable us to speak the truth; and may He take the veil from the hearts of those who are in error, and bring them and us to one mind in the reverent belief, and fervent love, of God's most holy Word!

[6] "Essays and Reviews," pp. 377. 404, Lond. 6th edit. 1861.

Prefatory remarks on Inspiration.

II. In dealing with this subject, let us first clearly understand, what we mean by the proposition, that the Scriptures are *inspired* by God.

1. We do *not* intend thereby to affirm, that the Writers of Holy Scripture were constrained to write, without any volition or consciousness on their part. David singing the Psalms was not like the Harp in David's hand. *He* was a *free agent, it* was a *mechanical instrument.* The Holy Ghost inspired the writers of Holy Scripture. *Holy men,* says St. Peter [7], *spake, being moved* or borne along [8] *by the Holy Ghost. All Scripture is given by inspiration of God,* says St. Paul [9]. It is animated by His Divine breath [1].

But while He inspired the Writers of Scripture, Almighty God did not impair their moral and intellectual faculties, nor destroy their personal identity.

Inspiration may be called a spiritual Transfiguration. At the Transfiguration of Christ on the Holy Mount, as described in the Gospels, Moses and Elias appeared in glory [2]. Moses the Giver of the Law was there, and Elias the greatest of the Prophets. They were transfigured. But Moses retained his identity; so did Elias. Moses was still Moses, and Elias was

---

[7] 2 Pet. i. 21.

[8] φερόμενοι, *carried along* like a ship by the wind, or like a vessel on a stream. In this text the Vatican Manuscript has ἐλάλησαν ἀπὸ Θεοῦ ἄνθρωποι, i. e. *men spake from God:* and this reading gives greater force to the assertion of their Divine Inspiration.

[9] 2 Tim. iii. 16. [1] θεόπνευστος.

[2] Matt. xvii. 2, 3. Luke ix. 30, 31. Cf. 2 Pet. i. 18.

still Elias. Each was recognized by the Disciples, Peter, James, and John.

So it is with the writers of Holy Scripture. Moses, when inspired, was raised above Moses uninspired. St. Peter, St. John, and St. Paul, when writing Holy Scripture, are lifted above themselves by the power of the Holy Ghost. They are raised above their own level, and that of this lower world, and are placed as it were on a "holy mount." They, from whose hands we have received the Law, the Prophecies, and the Gospels, are joined together with Christ on a Mountain of Transfiguration; they are illumined by His glorious light, and the cloud of His presence overshadows them; each of them retains his own personality, each shines in his own sphere; they are spiritualized and glorified; they are *transfigured*.

In the *written* Word of God there is a holy union of human with divine, and we are not able to draw the line, where what is human ends, and what is divine begins.

This union of human with divine in the *Written Word*, bears some resemblance to the greatest Mystery of our faith, the union of Man with God in the INCARNATE WORD. The Inspiration of Scripture may be compared to the Incarnation of Christ. Jesus Christ is *Emmanuel, God with us*[3], *God manifest in the flesh*[4]. The two natures of God and Man are joined together in His one Person. But

---

[3] Matt. i. 23.   [4] 1 Tim. iii. 16.

who would attempt to define the limits, where God's nature ends, and where Man's nature begins, in the Person of Christ? The union of God and Man in the *Incarnate Word* is a Mystery. So is the union of the Divine element with the human in the *Written Word*. It is a Mystery. In both cases the Mystery baffles all our powers of analysis. In both cases the Mystery, like the mid-day sun in the heavens, dazzles the eye with its brightness; we cannot gaze upon it. But, in both cases also, the Mystery, like the sun in the heavens, *enables us to see.* All would be dark in the moral and spiritual world, without the light of the Incarnate Word, and of the Written Word. And in both cases it is the union of Divinity with Humanity, which is the cause of spiritual light to the World [5].

Perhaps we may be allowed to illustrate this part of the subject by another comparison. Scripture is God's Word written. The things written are from God, and the Writing of them is from Him; *all Scripture is given by Inspiration of God.* The fresh and living Water of heavenly Truth issues from one Source, and that Source is Divine. But the water flows in various streams. The Fountain is Divine, the element is heavenly, but the channels are earthly, and the channels do not change the water, but they modify its direction and its course. The heavenly water acts upon the earthly banks of the streams; and the banks

---

[5] Some sentences are repeated here from the Preface to the Author's Edition of the Greek Testament, p. xviii. Second Edition, 1859.

act upon the water; they act and react upon each other with a simultaneous and concurrent operation. Sometimes the Divine element of Inspired Truth rushes vehemently in torrents and in cataracts, in the impetuous fervour of St. Paul. Sometimes it diffuses itself, and sleeps in calm and deep lakes, in the love and gentleness of St. John. The Element is one and the same, and Divine; the channels are different, and human; the power of the one destroys not the liberty of the other; Divine Grace does not annul the human intellect and will, though it is suggestive, preventive, suppletory, auxiliary to it, but the Divine Spirit, and the human Intellect and Will, concur and act together in loving harmony and joy.

2. We affirm, then, that there is a human element in Holy Scripture; but we assert also that this human element is refined, sublimed, spiritualized, and purified from all taint of human error, in the Word of God. We are not of those who say, that though Holy Scripture is inspired, it is marred and blemished by imperfections and inaccuracies. We cannot agree with some who assert, that the holy Evangelist St. Matthew errs in his exposition of the Prophecies recited in his first and second chapters. We cannot allow that St. Matthew and St. Luke are at variance with one another in their narratives of the incidents of our Lord's infancy; we cannot concede that St. Mark errs when he says that David ate the shewbread in the days of Abiathar

the High Priest⁶. We cannot admit, that St. Luke errs, in saying that the Taxing at the Nativity took place in the time of Cyrenius⁷. We cannot grant, that St. John errs, when he says that the Chief Priests had not eaten the Passover on the day of the Crucifixion⁸. We cannot concede that either he⁹ or St. Mark¹ errs in their record of the hour on which the Crucifixion took place. We know well, that all these allegations may be, and have been refuted. Having carefully examined the narratives of the four Evangelists, we deliberately affirm our conviction, that while there are sundry *varieties* serving to complete the Evangelical history, there is *no contradiction* in it².

Again; we cannot concur with those who say that there are historical mistakes in St. Stephen's speech to the Hebrew Sanhedrim³, and that therefore the Author of the Acts of the Apostles errs when he says that St. Stephen was *full of the Holy Ghost*, and that *no one could resist the wisdom and the spirit by which he spake*⁴. We cannot agree with those who affirm that St. Paul erred when writing to the Thessalonians, and speaking to them by *the Word of the Lord*⁵, and " entertained and expressed a belief which the event

---

⁶ Mark ii. 26.   ⁷ Luke ii. 2.
⁸ John xviii. 18.   ⁹ John xix. 14.
¹ Mark xv. 25.
² Cp. Euseb. Demonst. Evang. iii. 5, and S. Augustine's treatise De Consensu Evangelistarum.
³ Acts vii.   ⁴ Acts vi. 8—10.
⁵ 1 Thess. iv. 15. See " Essays and Reviews," p. 346.

did not justify," namely, that the Day of the Lord would come while he himself was still alive.

We are sure that these assertions, however confidently repeated, can never be proved.

We know that the Doctrines of Scripture are based on the History, and if the History is false, the Doctrines cannot stand. We know that the Bible is *for all*; it is for the simplest peasant as well as for the wisest philosopher, it is able to make all men *wise unto salvation*[6].

Not only are the *Writers* of Holy Scripture *moved by the Holy Ghost*[7], but the *writing* itself, every part of the whole *writing*, is described by St. Paul as filled with the breath of God[8]. The Book is inspired, and therefore the Scriptures are called *living* oracles[9], and are represented as *speaking*[1], and as endued with *foreknowledge*[2]. The Spirit of God animates them. They are saturated and bathed with the Divine Light. They become Light. *Thy word is a Lamp unto my feet, and a Light unto my paths*[3].

We cannot therefore admit that the Bible is blemished with errors, and that it is left for the reader "to separate by his own skill" what is erroneous in it from what is true. We know that the unbeliever may justly challenge those who make

---

[6] 2 Tim. iii. 15.   [7] 2 Pet. i. 21.
[8] πᾶσα γραφὴ θεόπνευστος, 2 Tim. iii. 16.
[9] Acts vii. 38.
[1] Mark xv. 28. John xix. 37. Rom. iv. 3; ix. 17; xi. 2. Gal. iv. 30.
[2] Gal. iii. 8.   [3] Ps. cxix. 105.

such an admission as that; and that he may fairly encounter them with the following language[4], "A book cannot be said to be inspired, or to carry with it the authority of being God's Word, if only *portions* come from Him, and there exists no plain and infallible sign to indicate *which* those portions are; and if the same Writer may give us in one verse of the Bible a revelation from the Most High, and in the next verse a blunder of his own. How can we be certain, that the very texts, upon which we rest our doctrines and our hopes, are not the *uninspired* portion? What can be the meaning or nature of an Inspiration to teach Truth, which does not guarantee its recipient from teaching error?"

3. In answer to such questions as these, we affirm that the Bible is the Word of God, and that it is *not marred by human infirmities*. We do not imagine with some that the Bible is like a Threshing-floor, on which wheat and chaff lie mingled together, and

---

[4] These paragraphs are transcribed from a Volume recently published by a sceptical writer, who reasons logically on the theory of those who say that the Bible is inspired and yet is blemished with error: and exposes the inconsistency of that theory. This sceptical writer, commenting on the admission made by an English Theologian that St. Paul "entertained a belief which the event did not justify" when he was speaking of the end of the world (1 Thess. iv. 13—18), observes very truly that "it is particularly worthy of remark, and seems to have been unaccountably overlooked" by that English Theologian "throughout his argument, that in the assertion of this so-called '*erroneous* belief, St. Paul expressly declares himself to be speaking by the *Word of the Lord.*'" For an elucidation of that text, and of those specified above in pp. 8, 9, the Author of these Lectures may perhaps be allowed to refer to the notes upon them in his edition of the Greek Testament.

that it is left for the reader to winnow and sift the wheat from the chaff by the fan and sieve of his own mind. We do not suppose that the Bible is like a rude mass, having threads and spangles of precious metal, intertwisted and encrusted in a mineral bed, and that it is left for the reader to smelt the ore from the dross. But we believe the Bible to *be pure gold. Every word of God is pure*[5]. We adopt the language of one of the wisest ancient divines[6],—"Such is the reverence I have learnt to pay to the Books of Holy Scripture, and to those Books alone, that I most firmly believe that none of those Writers has ever *fallen into any error in writing;* and if I find any thing in Scripture which seems to me at variance with the truth, I conclude that either my copy of the Bible is in fault, or that the translator has missed the sense, or that I have not rightly understood it[7]."

4. They who acknowledge that the Scriptures are inspired by the Holy Ghost, and yet assert that they

---

[5] Prov. xxx. 5. Cp. Ps. xii. 6; cxix. 140.

[6] *S. Augustine*, Epist. ad Hieron. 82; cp. *Irenæus* iii. 1, and iii. 5, where he speaks of the Apostles as having perfect knowledge (perfectam agnitionem) and placed beyond the reach of all falsehood 'extrà omne mendacium,' and so *Origen* (in Matth. tom. xvi. c. 12), "I believe that not a jot or tittle of the Gospels is without divine instruction; and that the Gospels were written with the co-operation of the Holy Ghost, and that they who wrote them never fell into an error." See also his Comment on John vi. c. 18; and Homil. in Num. xxvii. 1, where he says that in Holy Scripture there is 'nibil otiosum,' and (Homil. in Jerem. xxxix.), "there is nothing in Scripture which does not do its own proper work, if men know how to use it."

[7] See also *Hooker's* judgment on this subject in his Eccles. Polity, II. viii. 6.

are blemished by error, may be desired to consider, that if the Holy Ghost, who inspired the Scriptures, had not intended to preserve their writers from error, He would not have employed such persons as He did in writing the Scriptures. He would not have chosen *unlearned and ignorant men* [8], but the wise of this world. He would not have chosen a Galilæan fisherman, a hundred years old, for such St. John was, to write the record of the sublimest discourses of Jesus Christ. And if that Galilæan fisherman, and his brother Evangelists, being such as they were, had not been preserved from error by the Holy Ghost, they must have fallen into countless palpable errors, and manifest contradictions. But the Holy Spirit made choice of such feeble instruments with a wise design, in order that by the weakness of the instruments used, and by the perfection of the work done by their means, it might be seen and acknowledged by all, that the excellency of the Gospel written by their hands is *not of man, but of God* [9].

5. But while we thus affirm, that the genuine text of the Bible is free from error, we do not mean to assert that the persons employed to write the Bible, as Moses, the Prophets, and Apostles, were not liable to err. As *Writers* they were infallibly guided *in writing*, and were preserved from error by the Spirit of Truth, who inspired them, but they were

---

[8] Acts iv. 13.
[9] 2 Cor. iv. 7. Cp. Euseb. Demonst. Evang. iii. 5. Hist. Eccl. iii. 24.

14 *As men, the writers of Holy Scripture were fallible in practice;*

fallible *in practice as men.* They themselves confess this. *We are men of like passions with you*[1]. *In many things we offend all*[2]. The unerring word of Scripture records errors of the men, by whose instrumentality Scripture was written. *Moses spake unadvisedly with his lips*[3]. David the Psalmist laments the sins of David the King[4]. St. Luke in the Acts relates that St. Mark faltered for a season, and that St. Paul and St. Barnabas strove together concerning him[5]. St. Paul testifies that St. Peter *walked not uprightly*[6]. The unerring language of the Holy Spirit, writing by St. Paul in Holy Scripture, relates that St. Peter erred. We believe that St. Peter erred, because the Holy Spirit, who cannot err, asserts by St. Paul in Scripture that he did err[7]. But let us not confound the *Writers* with the *men.* Let us distinguish the *Writings* from the *practice* of those by whose hands they were written. Men they were, and being men, though holy men, they were liable to err. But the *Writings* which God the Holy Ghost dictated by their instrumentality, and which have been received as Holy Scripture by the Christian Church Universal, are exempt from error. And why? Because in writing they had the gift of the

[1] Acts xiv. 15.
[2] James iii. 2.
[3] Ps. cvi. 33.
[4] Ps. li.
[5] Acts xv. 37—39.
[6] Gal. ii. 11—14.
[7] This topic is admirably handled by S. Augustine in his correspondence with S. Jerome, Epist. xxviii. xl. and lxxxii.; as may be seen in the note on Gal. ii. 11, in the Author's Edition; cp. the note at the end of that chapter.

Holy Ghost who led *them into all truth* [8]. And their words were not such as *man's wisdom teacheth, but which the Holy Ghost teacheth* [9]; and, as St. Peter says, they *spake being moved by the Holy Ghost* [1]; and the Holy Ghost *is the Spirit of Truth* [2], and *every Scripture* [3], St. Paul declares, is *given by inspiration of God.* The workmen were human, but the work is divine. They had the *treasure* in *earthen vessels* [4], but the *treasure* itself is *not earthly*, but heavenly. The Channels, through which the water of Holy Scripture flows, are like the Roman aqueducts of brick or stone stretching across the Campagna, but the Water itself, which flows through them, is living water of salvation, streaming forth from the heavenly Hills, even from the pure wellspring of the Wisdom and Love of God.

6. Here also we may advert to those who allege that the language of the Apostles is not from God, because they sometimes speak *doubtingly. Inspiration is not Omniscience.* The Divine Spirit did not convert the Apostles into Divine beings. His aid was given to the Writers of Scripture according to the need. Sometimes it swelled the sails of their minds with a vehement gale; and at other times, when the oars of human toil, and the pilotage of human prudence, nearly sufficed for the purpose, would fan them only

---

[8] John xvi. 13.   [9] 1 Cor. ii. 13.
[1] 2 Pet. i. 21.   [2] John xiv. 17; xv. 26.
[3] πᾶσα γραφή, *every* Scripture (2 Tim. iii. 16).
[4] 2 Cor. iv. 7.

with a gentle breeze; sometimes it was almost lulled. He allowed the Evangelists to speak doubtingly in Scripture in some minor matters, where doubt was not hurtful; such as, for instance, in the capacity of the vessels of Cana [5], or in the number of furlongs which the Apostles had rowed [6]. He allowed St. Paul to avow, that whether he was in the body or out of the body, when he was caught up into the third heaven, he *could not tell* [7]; and to say that he *knows not* whether he baptized any besides those whom he mentions [8]; and He permitted him to express *doubts* concerning the future [9]. He inspired them to *inform* us of *their doubts* in these cases, in order that, in those other more momentous and mysterious matters, wherein they express *no doubt*, we might feel sure that they speak, not from themselves, but God.

7. Again. Doubtless there is a *perfect language* in *heaven*. But we may not allow ourselves to forget, that when God communicated the mysteries of Revelation to the world, in the pages of Holy Scripture, He did not speak in the tongues of Angels, nor did He create any new language, but He used a language already in being, a language formed by the ordinary intercourse of man with man, a language spoken in senates and law-courts, and streets and market-places

---

[5] John ii. 6.
[6] John vi. 19. Cp. xi. 18. Acts iv. 4. Luke ix. 28.
[7] 2 Cor. xii. 2.   [8] 1 Cor. i. 16.
[9] Rom. xv. 24. 1 Cor. xvi. 5, 6. 2 Cor. i. 15—17. Phil. ii. 19. 1 Tim. iii. 14.

of the world. Writing to men, He used the language of men. *The medium* by which He revealed the mysteries of the Gospel, was *ancient* and *human*, but what He revealed thereby was *novel* and *Divine*.

It is with Scripture as with Christ's Tribute-money [1]. The metallic ore, of which that money was made, was from God, it was dug up in the mine; and Christ by His miraculous power brought up the sum paid, from the depths of the sea: but the Coin itself, in which the sum was paid, had been struck in Cæsar's mint. So the substance of Scripture Doctrine is from God. Its mysteries are brought up from the abysses of Divine Wisdom. And the words in which it is taught, are words employed by God, through the ministry of Inspired men. But the language of which those words form a part, was framed by man; it was struck in a human mint; and like every thing human, by whomsoever used, that language was not free from imperfection; though doubtless the words, when used by men under the guidance of God, serve perfectly all the purposes, which God, in using them, intended them to serve. Almighty God did not destroy the writers' identity, He did not annul their free-will, but He used the writers aright. He did not create a new language, but He used the old with Divine Wisdom and Truth.

8. One more prefatory observation may be made here.

---

[1] Matt. xvii. 24—27.

It is sometimes alleged, that since the collation of the different Manuscripts of the Old and New Testament has brought to light an immense multitude of Various Readings, amounting to some hundreds of thousands, therefore, in this diversity of authorities, even *if* an inspired Text, and faultless Original, did exist any where, it would be impossible for us to find it out.

As to this objection from the multitude of Various Readings, this is not an evidence of uncertainty in the Sacred Text, but it is a proof of its *certainty*. The words of the original Scripture have been transcribed by human copyists, and though it may be allowed that no single copy, now existing, either of the Old or New Testament in their original tongues, exhibits precisely verbatim et literatim what was written by the Prophets and Apostles, yet it is certain that, by the collation of the copies which have been preserved, we have the Text of the Holy Scriptures in such a form, as may be depended on for all that we require, and that, in receiving that Text, we receive the Oracles of God.

For, let us consider; Whence does this multitude of Various Readings arise? From the multitude of copies. And this multitude of copies is the very thing which secures and proves the integrity of the Text. *If* there were only a few copies, there would be few Various Readings; and if there was only *one* copy, there would be *no* Various Readings at all. But then we should only have one witness to depend upon. But now we have many thousand witnesses, and since these witnesses *do vary* in some *very slight, trivial*, and *insignificant* matters, such as the chance omission of a word, or its transposition, or in a particle or conjunction, we see that there is no collusion, no conspiracy among the witnesses. And since they *agree in all substantial* respects, we are sure that what they witness is true; that is, that the Text, obtained by their aid, is correct, that it is a faithful representation of the Words dictated to the Prophets, Apostles, and Evangelists, by the Holy Spirit of God.

III. Let us now proceed to suppose that an unbeliever were to address us, and ask for a *reason* of the hope that is in us, when we assert our belief that the Bible is the Word of God. What answer should we give to that question?

If *that* belief is sound, there must be a reason for it. And since the Bible is for all, and all are bound to believe its doctrines and obey its precepts, it is clear that the answer to be given to this question ought to be of such a kind, that all, however unlearned, may be able to give it, and that all to whom it is given ought to be satisfied with it.

Suppose therefore that an unbeliever were to ask you this question, On what grounds do you believe the Bible, the whole Bible, and nothing but the Bible, to be the written Word of God?

1. Some persons have said, in reply to this in-

quiry, that *they themselves* have an *inward spiritual illumination*, by which they are enabled to discern the Bible to be God's Word. The Spirit in their hearts, they affirm, bears witness to the Spirit in the Bible, and assures them that it is His Word.

But is this answer adequate? Is it satisfactory?

Doubtless every devout person will feel, in reading the Bible, that he is reading no common book; he will feel his heart *burn within him* with holy love and joy, when he listens to its words, and when he observes also the harmony of the various parts of the Bible, and its adaptation to the needs of our nature, and the fulfilment of its prophecies; and when he reflects on the moral and social benefits conferred by the Bible on the world; and when he meditates on the wonderful dispensations of God's providence in protecting and preserving the Bible[2]. Every one who is really enlightened with divine grace will feel a strong persuasion that it *is* the Word of God.

2. But such considerations as these, important as they are, would not suffice to *convince an unbeliever* that the *whole* Bible is the Word of God. We need some other aid; and as for the appeal to our own individual consciousness, can it truly be said by any man, that, if portions of the Bible were interspersed with portions of an uninspired book,—such as the Book of Ecclesiasticus or of Wisdom,—and if, being thus blended together, they were placed before him,

---

[2] See below, Lecture V. pp. 102—114.

he could, by his own internal consciousness, discern and separate at once what is inspired from what is uninspired [3]?

We cannot admit this.

---

[3] Hooker says well on this point (Eccl. Pol. III. viii. 15):—" I doubt not but men of wisdom and judgment will grant, that the Church, in this point especially (the *Inspiration* of Holy Scripture) is furnished with reason, to stop the mouths of her impious adversaries; and that as it were *altogether bootless to allege against them* what the Spirit hath taught *us*, so likewise that even to our own selves it needeth caution and explication how the testimony of the Spirit may be discerned, by what means it may be known; lest men think that the Spirit of God doth testify those things which the spirit of *error* suggesteth. The operations of the Spirit, especially these ordinary which be common to all true Christian men, are, as we know, things secret and undiscernible even to the very soul where they are, because their nature is of another and an higher kind than that they can be by us perceived in this life. Wherefore albeit the Spirit lead us into all truth and direct us in all goodness, yet because these workings of the Spirit in us are so privy and secret, we therefore stand on a plainer ground, when we gather by reason from the quality of things believed or done, that the Spirit of God hath directed us in both, than if we settle ourselves to believe or to do any certain particular thing, as being moved thereto by the Spirit."

And Bishop Burnet (on the VIth Article) judiciously observes; In proof of the Inspiration of Holy Scripture, " I will not urge that of the testimony of the Spirit, which many have had recourse to: this is only an argument to him that feels it, if it is one at all; and therefore it proves nothing to another person; besides, the utmost that with reason can be made of this is, that a good man, feeling the very powerful effects of the Christian religion on his own heart, in the reforming his nature, and the calming his conscience, together with those comforts that arise out of it, is convinced in general of the whole of Christianity, by the happy effects that it has upon his own mind; but it does not from this appear, how he should know that such books and such passages in them should come from a Divine original, or that he should be able to distinguish what is genuine in them from what is spurious."

Private Consciousness no safe ground for belief in Inspiration.

We do well to believe the Inspiration of the Bible. But let those who would build their belief upon their own feelings, in this momentous matter, be affectionately entreated to consider, whether they may not haply be building on the sand. We need solid arguments to persuade *others*. We need strong *reasons* to convince the *unbeliever* that the *whole Bible is the Word of God*: he will not be satisfied with assertions, he will require proofs. Our perceptions are no rule for him. He will not ask for emotions, but evidences; he will require, not feelings, but facts. He may say to us, "*You* feel that the Bible is inspired, but *I* have no such feeling; and why should I rather be guided by *your* feelings in *receiving* the Bible, than you be swayed by *my* feelings in *rejecting* it? Besides, if I am to be influenced by men's sentiments, I should have as many different Bibles as there are different Religions. The Brahmin feels that a divine spirit speaks to him in the Vedas; the Mahometan hears a divine voice in the Koran; the Jew recognizes a divine presence in the Old Testament, but denies its existence in the New. And even among Christians some[4] receive the Apocryphal Books, such as the Books of Judith and Tobit, as divinely inspired, while others do not own them as such[5]. If personal feelings and opinions, apart from logical proofs, are to determine the matter,

---

[4] The Church of Rome. Concil. Trident. Sess. iv.
[5] The Church of England, Art. VI.

every form of Religion may have a separate Bible of its own, and there can be no common standard, no uniform Rule of Faith and Practice for all."

3. Consider, also, to what disastrous results this reference to private feelings and opinions in the solemn question of Inspiration, has already led.

That theory was first put forth at the Reformation in the sixteenth century by some pious men, to whom the world owed much. For example, to cite one of the greatest names of that time—Martin Luther said that he could not reconcile the doctrine of St. James with that of St. Paul, on the subject of Justification, and that *therefore*, inasmuch as he accepted the doctrine of St. Paul, he must reject the Epistle of St. James. In a similar temper he rejected the Book of Revelation of St. John the Divine. He did not *feel* their Inspiration; they were not congenial to his own opinions; they did not approve themselves to his mind. The Apostle St. Paul was inspired, because Martin Luther felt his inspiration. But the Apostles St. James and St. John were to wait, till the feelings of Martin Luther should change, for an allowance of their Inspiration. There is reason to believe that Luther lived long enough to rue this rash and reckless presumption[6]. But this example of arbitrary wilfulness, in dealing with Holy Scripture, did great mischief. Other Reformers, and even entire Reformed Churches[7],—happily *not*

---

[6] See Gerhardi Loci Theol. Appendix de Scr. Sacrâ, § 279 and § 299.

[7] Confessio Belgica v. Confessio Gallicana iv.

the Church of England [8],—grounded their recognition of Holy Scripture, and their belief in its Inspiration, upon what they called the internal witness of the Spirit in themselves. They resolved their belief into a mere private intuition, and personal assurance in their own hearts. They made themselves the judges of God's Word.

Here is the root of the evil which has now grown up into a great tree and overshadows Europe with darkness, and blights the vegetation beneath it, and yields deadly fruit. This internal Consciousness could only be an argument to the man who felt it, but could afford no conviction to others. They who rested their belief in the Bible on such a basis as that, could not defend the Bible against those who assailed it. Their belief in the Bible was true, but it rested on false grounds. It was built on the shifting quicksand of private opinion. As long as that inner Consciousness led them to acknowledge the Truth and Inspiration of the Bible, so long the unsoundness of their foundation did not manifestly appear. For some time they went on appealing to their own Consciousness, acknowledging the truth and divine origin of the Bible. But they were dwelling all the while in a tottering house; and ere long the storm came, and the house fell. Persons arose among them, who appealed to their own Consciousness, as a sufficient reason for *rejecting* the Bible.

---

[8] See below, Lecture IV. p. 90.

And they who had received the Bible on the assurance of their own supposed inner illumination, had no reply to offer to those who *rejected* it on similar grounds. The inner Consciousness of the one party was set in hostile array against the inner Consciousness of the other party. But who could arbitrate between them?

4. Thus in looking back to the history of Christendom, we see that the erroneous principle which was adopted by some pious men, *in support of the Bible*, three centuries ago, has now been applied by others *to destroy the Bible*. That erroneous principle has afforded a triumph to Infidelity.

The recently published volume, entitled "Essays and Reviews," which has startled and shocked the religious mind of the English Public, is only a natural fruit of the waywardness of private opinion developed in a sceptical direction. It has brought openly to the surface what has long been lurking beneath it; and if we are not wanting to ourselves, great good may be the result. The evil is now manifest. It displays itself in the light of day.

Relying on what they call "the verifying faculty" in their own minds, some impugn the veracity and genuineness of the Pentateuch, because they *think* that its records are inconsistent with the results of scientific research, or because they *suppose* its language to be posterior to the age of Moses. Some reject the Book of Daniel, because they *imagine* that its Prophecies were subsequent to the events which it professes to predict. Some will not receive the second Epistle of St. Peter, because the style of that Epistle differs from the First, and because they *think* that both those Epistles could not have been written by the same Author [9]. In short there is scarcely a single book in the Bible, which has not now been called into question by men who are swayed by their own feelings, and biassed by their own private opinions. "The nature of the Inspiration of Scripture," they say, "can only be shown from the examination of Scripture [1]," and whatever they find in the Bible *congenial to themselves*, whatever harmonizes with *their own sentiments, that* they believe to be inspired, and *that alone.* Thus the divinity of the Bible is made to depend on the fickleness of human caprice; and "unless God pleases man, He is to be no longer God [2]."

5. The Genuineness and Inspiration of the Bible

[9] Evidence of the truth of what is stated above, and much more to the same effect, may be seen in the Works of two German Writers, Hävernick's Einleitung in das Alte Testament, 1836—1849, and Guerike's Einleitung in das N. T., 1843. See also the valuable summary in the History of German Protestantism, pp. 100—134, by the Rev. E. H. Dewar, M.A., British Chaplain at Hamburgh, 1848. And before that time, the voice of warning had been raised by the late revered and beloved Hugh James Rose, in his Sermons preached before the University of Cambridge in 1824, and in the Appendix to them in 1828, and in his letter to the Bishop of London, 1829.

[1] "Essays and Reviews," p. 347. And again, "To the question, 'What is inspiration?' the first answer is, 'The idea which *we gather* from the study of it.' This is reconcileable with *variations* in *fact* in the Gospels ... with *inaccuracies of language* in the Epistles of St. Paul."

[2] *Tertullian*, Apol. c. 5. Nisi homini Deus placuerit, Deus non erit.

us a whole being thus made matter of doubt, the Bible itself is to be no longer the standard of Faith and Practice, but the varying consciousness of the individual is to be substituted in the place of God's holy Word.

6. Nor can there be any uniform standard of *Interpretation*, upon such principles as these. The Bible becomes like a rule of lead, which men may bend and twist aside according to their own will[3]. And thus they fall under St. Peter's censure, who says that *they that are unlearned and unstable wrest the Scriptures to their own destruction*[4].

IV. This condition of things is fraught with solemn warning and instruction. It teaches us that it is not enough to believe the truth, but that it is necessary to believe it on *right grounds*. If Belief is made to rest on a wrong foundation, it must give rise to Unbelief. It is not enough to believe that the Bible, the whole Bible, is God's written Word, but it is necessary to be able to *convince others* that this proposition is true. It is necessary to be always *ready to give to every man* that *asketh* us a *reason of the hope that is in us*.

Let us examine ourselves, whether we are able to do this. Let those who have hitherto built their

---

[3] Or, in the language of the poet Dryden,
"Their airy faith will no foundation find;
The Word's a weathercock to every wind."

[4] 2 Pet. iii. 16.

belief on the unsound basis of private feelings and private opinions, be earnestly entreated to contemplate the gigantic superstructure of error, which has now risen up in Europe upon that unsound basis. Let them be desired with words of tenderness and love,—to reconsider and revise their principles. The prevalence of Infidelity among us, the avowal of strange doctrines concerning the Inspiration of the Bible, which is the groundwork of all our hopes, imperatively demand this at their hands.

England is now on her trial. Now is the crisis of her religious life. If she has strength to eject the poison which has been infused into her, she may become more vigorous and healthy than before. But if not, then that poison will curdle in her veins, and her whole system will be diseased, and a moral mortification will ensue; and England will be in a few years, what some other Nations of Europe now are.

Let us, my beloved brethren, consider calmly the signs of the times; let us endeavour earnestly, by God's grace, to understand and maintain the truth; let us charitably and wisely labour to overcome evil with good. Then we may be sure, that the dangers, by which the Faith is now assailed, will prove means and occasions of new victories. Our difficulties are our opportunities. Our midnight is God's noon. Our trials may be our triumphs. They may conduce to heal our unhappy differences and dissensions, and to unite us all in the truth.

If the Bible is the unerring word of the Ever-living God; if, as we believe it is, it is the Universal Rule of Faith and Practice; if it is the Charter of our social and national privileges upon earth, and of our everlasting citizenship in heaven; if it is the Code, by which we shall be judged at the Great Day; then we may be sure, that all attacks upon it will one day recoil upon those who make them, like the foam and spray dashed from the firm-set rock. The violence of the storm will prove the strength of the fortress, and will confirm our belief in its impregnability, and in the faithfulness and power of Him, whose Divine Eye is ever upon it, and who shields it with the defence of His own Almighty protection. And thus, though the sea around us is tempestuous, *and though the waters thereof rage and swell,* yet in His own appointed time the *rivers of the flood thereof will make glad the city of God*[5].

With fervent hopes and earnest prayers for that blessed and glorious result, these introductory observations have been submitted to you on this subject; and it has been my endeavour to examine the principles which have been adopted by some, whose zeal for God's holy Word cannot be questioned, and to test the soundness of those principles by their results.

Time does not now allow us to consider on the present occasion, what is the *true foundation* on which

[5] Ps. xlvi. 2, 3.

the belief of the Inspiration of Holy Scripture is to be built; and what are the reasons by which we may hope to convince others, who do not now believe, that the Bible, the whole Bible, and nothing but the Bible, is the written Word of God.

This task will be undertaken in the Discourses that will be delivered in this Church on the Sunday Afternoons of the ensuing month. Brethren, let me entreat your prayers for God's help in this work, for His honour and glory, through Jesus Christ our Lord.

LECTURE II.

Romans iii. 1, 2.

What advantage then hath the Jew? Much every way: chiefly, because that unto them were committed the Oracles of God.

I. 1. In last Sunday's discourse we entered on the inquiry;

By what reasons are we persuaded, and by what arguments would we persuade others, that the Bible, the whole Bible, and nothing but the Bible, is the written Word of God?

It was then observed, that some pious persons have replied to this question by saying, that they themselves have an inward illumination, by which they are enabled to distinguish the Bible from all other books; and they rest their belief in the Inspiration of the Bible upon this private assurance.

But, as was then remarked, this assurance on *their* part cannot exercise any influence on *others*. Our belief in the Inspiration of the Bible cannot induce the *unbeliever* to receive it as God's Word.

It has also been already shown, that this appeal to private feelings and opinions, as the groundwork of belief in the Bible, has led to unhappy results. If we refer to our own feelings and opinions as an adequate proof of its Inspiration, we must not be surprised to find that other persons refer to *their* feelings and opinions, in *disproof* of it. When men make themselves to be the measures of truth, they are in great danger of losing the truth. They soon become entangled in a labyrinth of contradictions, and instead of strengthening the foundation of the Bible, they are like the builders of Babel, distracted with the strife of tongues.

2. It is scarcely necessary to add, that we cannot prove from *Scripture itself*, that Scripture is God's Word. The Holy Spirit says by St. Paul, that *all Scripture is given by inspiration of God*[1]. But it must *first* be *proved* by some arguments *external* to Scripture, as well as by *internal* evidence, derivable from Scripture, that St. Paul himself, when he wrote these words, wrote under the inspiration of God[2].

---

[1] 2 Tim. iii. 16.

[2] See Hooker, I. xiv. 1. "Of things necessary, the very chiefest is to know what books we are bound to *esteem holy;* which point is confessed impossible for *Scripture* itself to teach." And again, II. iv. 2, "It is not the Word of God which doth, or possibly can assure us that we do well to think that *is* His Word; for if any one Book of Scripture did give testimony to all, yet still *that* Scripture would require another to give credit to it; nor could we ever come to any pause to rest our assurance this way, so that unless *beside Scripture* there were something that might assure us that we do well, we could not think we do well, no not in being assured that Scripture is a sacred and holy rule of well-doing."

II. Let us now proceed to examine, what the *true* answer to the inquiry is?

Let us begin with the OLD TESTAMENT. On what grounds are we convinced, and by what proofs would we endeavour to persuade others, that the *whole* of the *Old Testament* is the Word of God?

1. First, we would reply, we receive the Old Testament as inspired, on the testimony of God, declared in the consent and practice of the Jewish Nation, to which, as the Apostle says, *were delivered*[a] *the Oracles of God*. St. Paul here affirms that the Ancient Jewish Church was the divinely constituted Recipient and Guardian of the Old Testament. Its testimony on this matter is the testimony of God.

2. Secondly, we receive the Old Testament as inspired on the Testimony of the Son of God Himself, our Blessed Lord and Saviour JESUS CHRIST.

First, then, we receive the Old Testament as inspired, on the testimony of God declared by the Jewish Nation.

III. Here we must begin by showing that the Old Testament, as it now exists in *our* age, is the same as the Old Testament in the first century of the Christian era: in other words, we must prove its *Integrity*.

---

[a] St. Paul's words are ἐπιστεύθησαν τὰ λόγια: a stronger phrase than that in our English Version. "They were *entrusted with* the oracles of God." They were the Trustees and Guardians of the Old Testament; and St. Paul would not have used this expression, if they had been unfaithful to that sacred trust.

This may be demonstrated from the fact, that the Old Testament has been *publicly read* both in Jewish Synagogues [4], and in Christian Churches [5], throughout the world, every week, from the first century to the present day.

The multiplication of copies of the Old Testament, for the purposes of this weekly public Reading in the Jewish Synagogues on the Jewish Sabbath, and in Christian Churches on the Lord's Day, and this public Reading itself, have served as providential guarantees for the preservation of the Old Testament.

Even if any of the Jews had ever desired to tamper with the Text of the Old Testament, they would have been prevented from effecting such a purpose by the diffusion of Copies of the Old Testament in all parts of the world [6]. Even if all the Jewish Synagogues had conspired together to alter the Text of the Old Testament, which is a thing incredible, they would have been hindered and checked from doing so by the counteracting vigilance of Christian Churches, guarding the Old Testament, and publicly reading the Old Testament in all parts of the civilized world.

And if, on the other side, any Christian Churches

---

[4] See on Acts xiii. 15; xv. 21. Josephus c. Apion. ii. p. 107½, and the authorities in Vitringa's treatise De Synagogâ Vetere, lib. iii. pt. 2, c. 8, p. 961, ed. Franck. 1696.

[5] See the authorities in Bingham's Antiquities, book xiv. ch. iii.

[6] See S. Augustine's observation on this point, de Civitate Dei, xv. c. 13.

had ever attempted to make any change in the Old Testament, such an attempt would have been exposed and frustrated by the Jews.

Thus we see, that under God's providential care for the Old Testament, even the rivalry and enmity of Jews and Christians have been overruled for good; they have been made instrumental in the preservation of His Holy Word, and in assuring the world of its integrity.

A Poet of old, speaking of a ship in a stormy night, says, "that in such a night it is good to have two Anchors cast out of the vessel;" one anchor from the prow, the other at the stern, in order that it may ride safely in the storm[7]. In the tempests of the long night of many centuries, the sacred vessel of Holy Scripture has been moored securely on the two Anchors of the Jewish Synagogue and of the Christian Church.

It is certain that the Old Testament, as it is now in the hands of the Jews dispersed every where, coincides exactly with the Old Testament in the hands of the Christian Churches diffused throughout the world.

This coincidence is an incontrovertible proof, that the Old Testament, which we have in our own hands at this day, is the same as the Old Testament in the first century of the Christian era.

IV. Let us, therefore, now ascend in our thoughts to the first century of the Christian era, and imagine

[7] Pindar, Olymp. vi. 172.

ourselves living then, and suppose the case of pious Israelites, such, for example, as an aged Simeon or a guileless Nathanael at that time.

By what arguments would they have been persuaded, and by what evidence would they have sought to persuade others, that the Old Testament which they had, is inspired by God?

1. Doubtless the first motive which impelled the devout Israelite to acknowledge the Old Testament as divine, was the fact that he saw it set apart from all other Books by the universal consent and uniform practice of his own Nation, to which God had vouchsafed wonderful marks of His favour and blessing.

He saw the Books of the Old Testament treated with pious reverence by the whole Hebrew People. He beheld those Books treasured up with devout care in the Synagogues, and brought forth, Sabbath after Sabbath, from the sacred chest in those Synagogues; he saw those Volumes unveiled, and unrolled with holy veneration; and before and after the reading of those Writings, he heard the accents of blessing and praise addressed to God for the gift of those sacred Writings, and he listened to their words recited with scrupulous care, and venerated with religious awe [s].

---

[s] The Jewish authorities, describing the forms and ceremonies used in the Synagogues, at the reading of the Old Testament, may be seen in the Treatise of Vitringa, De Synagogâ Vetere, lib. iii. pt. ii. cap. 8, pp. 961—975. See also the account of the reading of the Old Testament in the Synagogues, in Prideaux's Connexion, part i. book vi. on B C. 445—433.

Every Jew, from his infancy, was thus impressed with a belief in their Truth and Inspiration.

2. The feelings with which the pious Israelite regarded the Old Testament are thus described by a Writer living in the Apostolic age, who was eminently qualified to bear witness on this subject. That person is Josephus, the Jewish Historian, one of the most learned Authors of that time, a Pharisee, and of a priestly family, and descended from the Asmonean Princes. He speaks of the Old Testament as follows[9]: "We Jews have not a multitude of books at variance with one another," as the Heathen have, "but we have only Twenty-two Books." Such was the reckoning of the Jews, by whom several Books of the Old Testament were counted as one; for instance, the Twelve Minor Prophets were reckoned by them as one Book[1], and so, on the whole, their Twenty-two Books, beginning with Genesis and ending with Malachi, correspond to our Books of the Old Testament. "We have only Twenty-two Books, which contain the record of all time, and are *the Books* which are rightly *believed to be divine*. Five of these are the Books of Moses, which comprise our Laws, and the history of the human race until the death of Moses."

Josephus then proceeds to describe the other Books of the Old Testament; and sums up his account with these memorable words;—"We show by our

---

[9] Josephus c. Apion. i. § 8.
[1] See Bp. Cosin on the Canon of Scripture, chap. ii.

practice, what our belief is in these Books. For, although so long a time has elapsed since these Books were written, yet no one has ever ventured to make any addition to them, nor to take any thing from them, nor to make any change in them. And it is a principle innate in every Jew, to *regard these Books as Oracles of God, and to cleave to them; yea and to die gladly for them.*"

3. Such, then, was the judgment of the Jewish Nation concerning the Old Testament.

On what proofs did this judgment rest?

First, the Diffusion of those Books into all parts of the world, and the weekly public Reading of them for many centuries in Synagogues before the Christian era, had secured them inviolate. The Translation also of those Books into the Greek language[2], and the multiplication of copies in that language was another safeguard. The formation of Chaldee Paraphrases of the Old Testament served also for a similar purpose.

4. Even the greatest national *afflictions* of the Hebrew People had been made by God to subserve His gracious purposes in guarding, preserving, and disseminating His own Word, and in assuring the world of its Integrity.

In the age of King Rehoboam, the son of Solomon, Ten Tribes of Israel had revolted from the House of Judah[3], and they always remained separate from the

---

[2] See Josephus, Antiquities xii. 2. 4—15.
[3] 1 Kings xii. 16—19.

Two Tribes of Judah and Benjamin. Israel and Judah were split asunder, and formed two rival kingdoms. This was a great calamity, but God educed good from it: the one kingdom acted as a check on the other in the custody of the Bible. Though these kingdoms were opposed to each other in other respects, yet they agreed in receiving the same Bible. Thus under God they co-operated in the guardianship of His Word.

If King Jeroboam and his successors on the Throne of Israel, and the Ten Tribes who were subject to them, had been able to convict the Two Tribes of making any alteration in the Old Testament, they would not have failed to do so. The Kings of Israel, after its defection from Judah, set up rival objects of worship at Dan and Beersheba; and they would have drawn off more worshippers from Jerusalem to their own altars, and have strengthened their own secular power, if they could have alleged with truth that the Two Tribes had been faithless to their trust, and had tampered with the Word of God. And *if*, on *their* side, the *Ten Tribes* had made any change in the text of the Old Testament, the *Two Tribes* would have raised their protest against such alteration.

The fact however is, that the Ten Tribes and the Two Tribes, though severed from each other by many religious jealousies, and political antipathies, had but one and the same Bible. Though *Ephraim envied Judah*, and *Judah vexed Ephraim*[4], yet Ephraim and

---
[4] Isa. xi. 13.

Judah agreed in receiving and revering the same Scriptures. And though in course of time the Ten Tribes were carried away captive [5] beyond the Euphrates, and were scattered abroad in Media and Persia, and also in Asia and Egypt; and though afterwards the Two Tribes also were taken away [6] from their own home to Babylon and to other cities of the East, yet all the Twelve Tribes, wherever dispersed throughout the world, were united as one man in the reading of the same Scriptures; and they have maintained that union inviolate even to this hour [7].

V. This universal reception and public reading of the Old Testament is also a proof of its *Truth*.

Consider the contents of the Old Testament. Open the Bible. Examine the Pentateuch, or five Books of Moses. They do not give a flattering representation of the Hebrew Nation. On the contrary, they exhibit it in a very unfavourable light. They display the Israelites as rebelling against God immediately after they had been rescued from Egypt, and when He was doing mighty works in their

---

[5] 2 Kings xvii. 6.   [6] 2 Kings xxiv. 10; xxv. 11. 20.

[7] The case of the Samaritan Pentateuch supplies no exception to this statement. The Samaritans were foreigners (see Luke xvii. 18, and cp. Hengstenberg, die Authentie des Pentateuches, p. 4), and not Israelites. And the coincidence of the Samaritan Pentateuch with the Hebrew affords a remarkable testimony to the integrity of the latter. See Walton, Prolegomena, cap. xi. The allegation that there are interpolations in the Pentateuch, which are later than the age of Moses, is examined and refuted by Hävernick, § 134, pp. 541—9 of the original work, or pp. 361, 362 of the English Translation, 1850. Cp. Hengstenberg, die Authentie des Pentateuches, vol. ii. pp. 179—338.

behalf, and showering down favours upon them. If, as some allege, the Author of the Pentateuch had been writing a fictitious account of miracles that had never been wrought, and of mercies that had never been vouchsafed, he would have said that all the People were so astounded by the stupendous majesty of the miracles, and were so affected by the gracious beneficence of the mercies, that they were riveted by them in unswerving obedience.

But no; Moses displays to us the Hebrew Nation as falling into idolatry in the wilderness, after their deliverance from their enemies, and when God was about to give them the Law from Mount Sinai[8]. He exhibits them rebelling against God, when He was feeding them with bread from heaven, and giving them water from the rock[9], and leading them with a pillar of fire[1]. At the close of the forty years' sojourn in the wilderness, just before his death, his testimony of them is, *Ye have been rebellious against the Lord, from the day that I knew you*[2]. The Pentateuch is a censure upon Israel. St. Stephen, speaking in the Name of Jehovah, sums up its history, *O ye house of Israel, have ye offered to Me slain beasts and sacrifices by the space of forty years in the wilderness? Yea, ye took up the tabernacle of Moloch, and the star of your God Remphan, figures which ye made to worship them: and I will carry you away beyond Babylon*[3].

[8] Exod. xxxii. [9] Exod. xvi. 2; and xvii. 2.
[1] Exod. xiv. 20.
[2] Deut. ix. 24. The whole Chapter is very important in this light.
[3] Acts vii. 42—44.

The Books of Moses also relate, that on account of their sins, all the Israelites that came out of Egypt, with the exception of two, were excluded from the Land of Promise[4]. Thus the Author frankly confesses the insufficiency of his own guidance and government to bring them into that Land, and implies a failure on his part.

He also honestly records his own sin, and his consequent exclusion from Canaan[5]. He relates the sin of his brother Aaron[6] in making the golden calf; and the sin of his sister Miriam[7] in murmuring against himself; and the sin of his brother's sons Nadab and Abihu[8], for which they were destroyed by God; and the sin of some of his own Tribe, Korah and his company, for which they were consumed by fire[9].

Men are prone to speak well of themselves, and to eulogize their own nation. No man, it may be safely affirmed, writes libels on himself, and on his own family, and on the people committed to his rule. Nations are wont to dress up and embellish their own History in terms flattering to themselves. But no Nation has ever adopted calumnies against itself, and publicly recited them, in all parts of the world, and venerated them as oracles of God.

But the Hebrew People *has* accepted the Pentateuch as its own History written by the hand of

---

[4] Deut. i. 35, 36. 38.
[5] Numb. xx. 12.
[6] Exod. xxxii.
[7] Numb. xii. 1.
[8] Levit. x. 1.
[9] Numb. xvi.

God. It has read it publicly as such ever since it was written.

The great National yearly Festivals to which the Jews resorted from all parts of the world, were also standing monuments of the historical veracity of the Pentateuch. The Passover, Pentecost, and Tabernacles, at which the Pentateuch was publicly read in the ears of all the people every seventh year [1], commemorated the wonderful facts, recorded by Moses in the Pentateuch, and bore witness to its truth.

Therefore we may justly conclude that the Pentateuch is *true*.

VI. 1. The devout Israelite, being thus convinced of the *Integrity and Truth* of the Pentateuch, would next proceed to the proof of its *Inspiration*.

In that true History he saw his own Nation set apart by God, from ancient days, as a holy People. He knew from that History that the Tabernacle [2] in the wilderness had been fenced off by God from other places. He knew that in that Tabernacle there was a place distinguished from the rest, and called the Holy of Holies. He knew that in the mysterious darkness of that Holy of Holies, separated by the Veil, which hung before it, was the Ark; and, above the Ark, the Mercy Seat; and on the Mercy Seat the Cherubim, stretching their wings over it; and that this Mercy Seat was the Dwelling-place of the Divine Presence, and into that most Holy Place

---

[1] Deut. xxxi. 10.   [2] Exod. xxv. 8—22; xxvi. 33.

no one might enter, except the High Priest, and he only once a year[3].

2. Observe now the visible and practical testimony thus afforded by God Himself to the *Inspiration* of the Old Testament.

As soon as the Pentateuch was written, He commanded Moses to place it in the Holy of Holies, by the side of the Ark, the Throne of God[4]. God Himself thus set apart *that* Book from all other books. He declared that it is *not* "a common book." He enshrined it in His own Oracle, He consecrated it. The God of Truth Himself thus avouched its veracity. The Omnipotent thus protected it. He received it under *the shadow of His Wings* and made it *safe under His feathers*[5]. The Holy One of Israel thus also proclaimed its sanctity. He acknowledged it as His own.

This Book of the Law, treasured up in the Holy of Holies, was the Original, from which Copies were to be made; and it was the standard by which those copies were to be revised and verified. The sacred Original was to remain in the most Holy Place. But

---

[3] Levit. xvi. 2. 32.

[4] See Deut. xxxi. 9. 24—26. Josh. xxiv. 26. That this command concerned the whole Pentateuch is clearly shown by Hävernick, Einleitung i. p. 19. The objection of some recent sceptical writers (such as De Wette and others), alleging that this statement is inconsistent with the assertion in 1 Kings viii. 9, that in Solomon's days there was nothing in the Ark save the Two Tables of stone, is refuted by the fact that the Law is *not* said in Deut. xxxi. 26, to be deposited *in* the Ark, but *by the side* of it. Cp. Josephus, Antiq. viii. 4.

[5] Ps. xci. 4.

the knowledge of its contents was to be diffused every where.

In order still further to declare its divine authority, Almighty God commanded that the Kings of the Hebrew Nation should make with their own hands a copy of the Law from the Original that was kept in the Holy of Holies [6]. Sovereigns were to be its transcribers, and to keep the Law of God always by their side, as the code and charter of their government [7].

This sacred Original was preserved in the Tabernacle, and in the Temple, for many generations [8]; and in all probability it was this Original, which, having been rescued from the hands of idolatrous Princes, and secreted in evil days, was discovered in the Temple in the days of the good King Josiah [9]. It was the sight of that venerable Volume, written by the great Lawgiver, and the sound of the divine words recited from that holy oracle, which affected the tender heart of that pious youthful Prince with awe and penitential sorrow for the sins of the People committed to his charge, and with godly fear of the divine judgments hanging over their heads.

3. The truth of the *Pentateuch* being proved, and

---

[6] Deut. xvii. 18, 19. Josh. i. 8.

[7] Cp. the remarks of Hävernick, Einleitung, § 139 of the original, or § 35 of the English Translation.

[8] See preceding page.

[9] 2 Chron. xxxiv. 14, 15. 2 Kings xxii. 8—10. See Bishop Patrick and Dr. Kennicott on 2 Kings xxii. 8, and Hävernick's Einleitung, § 139, or § 35 of the English Translation.

its Inspiration being avouched, it follows as a necessary consequence that the *rest of the Old Testament* is also divinely *inspired*.

The Old Testament was called "*the Law, and the Prophets*[1]," and it is certain that all the Jews regarded the *Prophets* as on a par with the *Law*. They revered *the Law and the Prophets* as the lively oracles of God.

Almighty God had commanded in the *Law*, that if any man laid claim to be called a *Prophet* of the Lord, and could not establish that claim, he was to be put to death[2].

Thus God had provided a safeguard against the reception of any prophecy, which could not *prove its divine origin*. And since the *Prophetical Books* of the Old Testament *were* received universally by the Hebrew Nation as of *equal authority* with the Books of the *Law*, which were enshrined by God's command in the Holy of Holies, this concurrent consent of God's people is no other than the witness of God Himself to the Divine Authority of the Prophets.

Consider, also, that the Hebrew Prophets do not flatter the Hebrew People. They speak with holy boldness, as Ambassadors of God, in stern and severe language, and rebuke them for their sins, and call them to repentance, and denounce divine retribution upon them, unless they repent. God's commission to them was, *Cry aloud, spare not, lift up thy voice*

---

[1] See Matt. xxii. 40. Luke xvi. 16. Acts xiii. 15.
[2] Deut. xiii. 5; xviii. 20. Cp. Jer. xiv. 15. Zech. xiii. 3.

like a trumpet, and show *My people their transgression, and the House of Jacob their sins* [3].

Can it be supposed by any reasonable man, that the Hebrew People would have received such writings as theirs, and would have revered them as of equal authority with the Books of Moses, unless they had been constrained by the most cogent proofs and irresistible arguments to acknowledge their divine authority? No. They would have treated them in the same scornful and contumelious manner as the unhappy King Jehoiakim, sitting in his winter-house with the fire burning on the hearth, treated the Prophetic Roll of Jeremiah [4]; they would have cut them into shreds, and have destroyed them. But no: they did not dare to do so. They received them; they bowed their heads before them with reverential awe, and acknowledged them to be the oracles of God.

Thus even the sins of the Jews have been made instrumental in proving the Inspiration of the Old Testament. Their sins, by which they broke the commands contained in the Old Testament, show that, if they had been able, they would have rejected those Books by which their sins are condemned. But they received them as divine. They carry them every where in their hands. Even to this day they wander about, a National Cain, having killed their

---

[3] Isa. lviii. 1.   [4] Jer. xxxvi. 22.

own brother Abel—the true Shepherd of the sheep, and bear about with them the mark of God[5].

4. Here also we have another proof that no alteration has ever been made in the Old Testament. The Prophets of God rebuke the People for their sins. But the Prophetical Books do not contain a single syllable of reproof addressed to the Jewish People for the sin of altering their Scriptures. *If* the People had ever committed so heinous a sin as that, it must have been noticed by the Prophets. And since those Books do not give any hint that any such alteration was ever attempted, we may rest assured, that the Hebrew Scriptures were preserved inviolate by the Hebrew People.

VII. Let us now fix our eyes on the historical epoch when those Scriptures were completed. This was after the return of the Jews from Babylon; in the time of Ezra, about 440 years before Christ.

Almighty God then raised up holy men, who revised the copies of the Old Testament, and were commissioned to add some writings to them, and to seal up the Scriptures, and to deliver them to future ages. Ezra himself, *the Priest of God and Scribe*[6], was one of these; and with him were the Prophets Haggai, Zechariah, and Malachi, whose divine mission has been proved by the fulfilment of their

---

[5] Gen. iv. 15.   [6] Ezra vii. 6. 10. 12.

Prophecies. The sacred Volume was then closed[7]. Malachi is called by the Jews "the Seal of the Prophets." The voice of Prophecy ceased with him, and it remained silent for four hundred years, when it sounded forth again with clear accents at the coming of Christ.

VIII. The pious Israelite, who meditated on these facts, would see strong reason to remain stedfast in the belief of his forefathers, that the Books of the Old Testament were given by Inspiration of God. And when he examined the contents of those Scriptures, the more he would be convinced that this belief is true. The beauty, majesty, and simplicity of the Hebrew Scriptures; their adaptation to the nature and needs of mankind; the holiness of their precepts, the harmony of all their parts, extending through a thousand years, the fulfilment of their

---

[7] See Josephus c. Apion. i. § 8, and the assertions of the Hebrew Rabbis in the Mishna, tom. iv. p. 409, ed. Surenhusii, Amst. 1702, and Buxtorfii Tiberias, capp. x. and xi. pp. 90—99, ed. Basil. 1665. Prideaux's Connexion, part i. books v. and vi. Bp. Beveridge on the VIth Article, p. 271, ed. Oxf. 1840, and Hävernick, Einleitung, § 8, pp. 27—38, and Dr. W. Lee on Inspiration, p. 302.

Ezra, Haggai, Zechariah, and Malachi *revised* the copies, and closed the Canon of the Old Testament. But the notion that Ezra *restored* the Old Testament, after it had been destroyed, is an apocryphal fable. Some ancient Christian Fathers are cited in support of it. Irenæus iii. 21. Cp. Euseb. H. E. v. 8. Clemens Alex. Strom. 1. xxii. Tertullian de cultu mulier. c. 3. S. Jerome c. Helvid. c. 3. But they do not maintain it. The work de mirab. Script. (ii. 33) ascribed to S. Augustine, and quoted by some as countenancing that fable, is spurious. The Christian Fathers bear testimony to the genuine Jewish tradition that Ezra and the Prophets with him revised and completed the Canon of the Old Testament.

prophecies, the blessings conferred on those who received and obeyed them, would establish him more firmly in that faith.

IX. This faith of the ancient people of God is *our* faith also: we receive the Old Testament from the hands of those, to whom, as the Apostle says, *were committed the oracles of God*.

A few words may be said here, in reply to a sceptical objection.

"You say that you receive Moses, David, and Isaiah, on the testimony of the Jews; but did not the Jews reject Jesus Christ? What rational ground," we are asked, "can you assign for disregarding the decision of the Jews in the case of Jesus, and accepting it submissively in the case of Moses, David, and Isaiah[8]?"

To this question it may be replied, that the pious and devout Jews, who received Moses, David, and Isaiah, did *not* reject Jesus Christ. Nay rather, *because* they received the Prophets, therefore they received Jesus Christ. Their language was, *We have found Him of Whom Moses and the Prophets did write, Jesus of Nazareth the son of Joseph*[9].

True it is, that some Jews who held the Old Testament in their hands, but did not *understand the voices of the Prophets, which were read in their synagogues every Sabbath day, fulfilled them in condemning*

---

[8] These words are transcribed from a Volume recently published by a sceptical writer.
[9] John i. 45.

Him[1], and thus, even by their unbelief, they proved the Truth and Inspiration of those Prophets. For, those Prophets had foretold, that many of the Jews to whom the Prophecies concerning Christ were delivered, would not understand and believe them. For example, Isaiah asks, when prophesying of Christ, *Lord, who hath believed our report*[2]? He *anticipates unbelief.* Wonderful indeed it was, that the unbelieving Jews fulfilled those Prophecies, by doing those very things to Jesus Christ which those Prophecies foretold that they would do[3]. Thus the Unbelief of those who *fulfilled* those Prophecies by rejecting Christ, is an argument for the truth of those Prophecies, and it is a proof of the wisdom of those who understood those Prophecies and received Him.

Indeed, here is another evidence of God's Divine power in preserving the Scriptures, and of Christ's truth, concerning whom those Scriptures speak. We Christians receive Jesus Christ on the evidence of those Prophecies which are guarded by Jews who reject Christ. Therefore it cannot be alleged by the adversaries of Christianity, that we have tampered with the documents by which we prove its truth. Those documents come to us from the Jews. We appeal to the Old Testament, which is preserved by them who hold no converse with us. The Jews, even

---

[1] Acts xiii. 27.
[2] Isa. liii. 1. See St. John's comment on that passage of Isaiah. John xii. 38.
[3] Acts xiii. 27.

to this day, guard the Title-deeds of Christ whom they have crucified. From the words of Moses, David, and Isaiah, in their hands, we prove the Divine mission of Jesus Christ [f].

X. Let us now review what has been said. As soon as the Pentateuch was written, God provided for its safe custody. He enshrined it in the Holy of Holies, and placed it under the wings of the Cherubim. Thus God Himself declared it to be divine. That Book was a precious jewel set in a holy casket by His hand. Copies were to be made of it. Kings were to write them. "The Holy Spirit spake by the Prophets," and added their writings to the Law of Moses. The divine Institution of the weekly Sabbath, and of the yearly National Festivals, promoted the study of the Law, and bare witness to its truth. The dispersion of the Levites as the Expositors of the Law, throughout the Holy Land; and the raising up of Prophets, who were God's Messengers, were providential arrangements for preserving the Old Testament, and for assuring the People of its divine authority. The national calamities of the Hebrew People were made subservient to the same end. The dissolution of the Twelve Tribes into two separate kingdoms, and the downfall of those King-

---

[f] This argument is eloquently urged by S. Justin Martyr, Cohortat. ad Græcos, cap. 13, and by S. Augustine in Psalm. xl. and lvi. Proferimus codices ab inimicis ut confundamus alios inimicos. Codicem portat Judæus, unde credat Christianus. Librarii nostri facti sunt. See also his treatise c. Faustum, xii. c. 13, and de Unitate Ecclesiæ, c. 16.

doms, and the dispersion of the Ten Tribes and of the Two Tribes into all parts of the world, where Synagogues were built for the reading of the Scriptures on the Sabbath days; and the universal consent of all those scattered Tribes, receiving the same Bible and venerating it as the Word of God, have also been instrumental in guarding and diffusing the Old Testament, and in guaranteeing its integrity and truth.

These divine dispensations are clear evidences of design. They are witnesses of a providential superintendence, watching over the Old Testament for fifteen hundred years from the days of Moses to those of Christ. Almighty God speaks by them, and proclaims the integrity, the veracity, and the inspiration of the Old Testament.

This testimony extends to the whole of the Old Testament. It covers the entire Volume.

That providential care has been also continued from the age of Christ to this hour,—that is, for near two thousand years. Even the rejection of Christ by the Jews, and their hostility to Christianity, have been made ministerial to the custody of the Scriptures, and to the proof of their Truth and Inspiration.

The care with which God has guarded the Books of the Old Testament has not been relaxed for a moment since they were written. He that watcheth over them *neither slumbers nor sleeps* [5]. Nay rather,

[5] Ps. cxxi. 4.

that providential care has manifested itself more clearly in every successive age.

The Pentateuch was placed in the Holy of Holies and was enshrined under the wings of the Cherubim. And now,—as we shall proceed to show,—the *whole* of the OLD TESTAMENT has been placed under the protection of the INCARNATE WORD. It is safe under the guardianship of JESUS CHRIST, *Who is the same yesterday, and to-day, and for ever*[6]. And thus the conclusion at which we have arrived—namely, that the whole of the Old Testament is the inspired Word of God—is more firmly strengthened and established.

This is what will be proved, with God's help, in the next discourse.

[6] Heb. xiii. 8.

LECTURE III.

Luke iv. 14—17.

And Jesus returned in the power of the Spirit into Galilee: and there went out a fame of Him through all the region round about.

And He taught in their Synagogues, being glorified of all.

And He came to Nazareth, where He had been brought up: and as His custom was, He went into the Synagogue on the Sabbath day, and stood up for to read. And there was delivered unto Him the Book of the Prophet Esaias.

On what grounds do we receive the whole of the Old Testament as the inspired Word of God?

I. To this question one answer has been already given;—We receive the whole of the Old Testament as such, on the authority of God Himself declared by the universal consent and practice of His own People, the Jews, to whom, as St. Paul says, *were committed the oracles of God*[1], that is to say, who were *entrusted* with the guardianship of the Books of the Old Testament.

II. Let us now proceed to show, that this testimony to the Inspiration of the Old Testament, is confirmed

---

[1] Rom. iii. 1.

and verified by the infallible witness of our Lord and Saviour JESUS CHRIST. The INCARNATE WORD Himself sets his own divine seal on the written Word. The Son of God delivers to us all the Books of the Old Testament as the inspired Oracles of God. He who is *the Way, the Truth, and the Life*[2], proclaims that these Books show to us the Way of Salvation, and that they are words of Truth, and will lead all who receive them, with faith in Himself, to the joys of Life Eternal.

Hence we may derive a firm assurance, which cannot be gainsaid, that the whole of the Old Testament is the inspired Word of God.

But, it may be asked,

How is this proposition proved?

Why do we receive this testimony of Christ? Why do we appeal to that testimony as a sufficient ground for our own belief in the Inspiration of the Old Testament?

III. In order to answer that question, we must *begin* with taking into our hands the *Four Gospels*, which profess to relate the sayings and actions of Jesus Christ.

1. We can prove by *external* testimony, that these *Four Gospels* existed, in the same state as that in which they now exist, at the end of the first century of the Christian era, that is, nearly 1800 years ago. Ancient authors testify, that St. John's Gospel was

---

[2] John xiv. 6.

written at that time, and that he acknowledged the truth of the other three Gospels,—those of St. Matthew, St. Mark, and St. Luke,—and added his own Gospel, to complete the Evangelical History [3].

2. We can also prove by *external* evidence, that those Gospels, thus completed by St. John, were received, and were publicly read [4] as *true Histories*, by large communities of men, who had the best opportunities of testing and knowing their truth; namely, by the Christians, and by the Christian Churches which existed in primitive times. They never would have read those Gospels unless they had believed them; they never would have believed them unless those Gospels were true.

We can show that those persons and Churches could not have been deceived as to the credibility of those Gospels. We can show that they could not have deceived others. They were plain simple men. They had no human learning, wealth or power. We can show that they had no earthly interest to serve in asserting the truth of those Gospels. The assertion of that truth exposed them to the loss of all worldly things. They resisted all earthly tempta-

---

[3] See Clemens Alexandrin. ap Euseb. vi. 15; cp. Euseb. iii. 24. Canon Muratorian. in Routh's Reliquiæ Sacræ, iv. p. 2. Victorin. in Apocalyps. Bibl. Patr. Max. iii. 41. Theodor. Mopsuest. in Catenâ ad Joann. in Dr. Mill's Greek Test. p. 198.

[4] Irenæus iii. 1; iii. 11. 7—9. See Justin Martyr. Apol. i. 67. Cp. Westcott on the Canon of the New Test. p. 365 and p. 367: "No one at present will deny that they (the Gospels, &c.) occupied the same position in the estimation of Christians in the time of Irenæus (i. e. in the second century) as they hold now."

tions; they endured, cheerfully endured, all privations, sufferings, and torments for its sake [5]. They were stoned, beheaded, crucified, burnt, cast to the wild beasts. These things, and more, they suffered in defence of the Truth of the Four Gospels.

3. Now mark the wonderful result.

That very Power, the Power of Rome, Heathen Rome, Imperial Rome, which at first persecuted the Christians, and beheaded the Christians, and crucified the Christians, and cast the Christians to wild beasts for asserting the truth of the Gospels; that very Power itself, that Roman Power, that Heathen Power, that Imperial Power, that Power which then ruled the world, was itself at length convinced of the Truth of the Four Gospels, which were received as God's Word by the Christians. That self-same Roman Power, the Queen and Mistress of the World, was converted to the cause of the Gospels. She publicly owned her conversion; she acknowledged

---

[5] Especially in the persecution under the Roman Emperor Diocletian, A.D. 303, who endeavoured to destroy the copies of the Christian Scriptures, and burnt many of those writings. See Euseb. Hist. Eccl. viii. 2. Lactant. de mort. Persecutor. c. xii. The Christians who were tempted by fear to surrender copies of them to their heathen persecutors were called "traditores" by their brethren. See the Passio of S. Felix in Baluzii Miscellanea ii. p. 77. Gieseler, Church Hist. § 55 and 56. Routh, Reliquiæ Sacræ, tom. v. p. 348. "The holy Martyrs in their Acts (collected by Ruinart, Amst. 1713, see pp. 87. 89. 356, 357. 394) proclaim in the presence of their Judges, that the Holy Books received by the Christians at that time,—the Gospels and the other Books,—are revered by them, and are believed to be directly inspired, and are affectionately guarded by them unto death, and are not to be given up to any one."

that those whom she had put to death as Christians, were Martyrs to the Truth. She revered the memories of Peter and Paul whom she had killed. She who by the force of arms had made the Nations of the world to pass under her military yoke, humbly and meekly bowed her own head beneath the yoke of Christ. She changed her magnificent Heathen Temples into Christian Churches. And in those Heathen Temples, when changed into Christian Churches, the Four Gospels of Matthew and Mark, Luke and John were thenceforth read as true and divine histories. She placed those Four Gospels upon Thrones in her own Council Chambers [6]; and the Cross of Jesus of Nazareth, who had been crucified by the Roman Governor Pontius Pilate,—yes, the Cross of Jesus of Nazareth, of obscure Nazareth, in despised Galilee,—dislodged the Roman Eagle from the military Standards of the Roman Legions, and was set on the Imperial Diadem of the Roman Masters of the world.

These are facts as clear as the noonday sun. And in the face of these facts, who will venture to come forward and say that the Four Gospels are not *true?*

4. This proposition then being admitted, that the Gospels are *true*, it follows, as a logical inference,

---

[6] The Emperor Constantine thus speaks in his oration to the Bishops at Nicæa : " The Gospels and the Apostolic writings and the oracles of the ancient Prophets clearly teach us what to believe of God. Let us receive the solution of the question before us from the *divinely inspired words* (ἐκ τῶν θεοπνεύστων λόγων)." Theodoret, 1. 5.

that our Lord Jesus Christ did indeed perform those wonderful works, which He is related in the Four Gospels to have done; that in the presence of great multitudes,—many of them His bitter enemies,—He healed the sick, cast out devils, raised the dead; that He knew the thoughts and searched the hearts of men, and foretold future events; that He rose again from the dead, and ascended into heaven: in a word, that He displayed power, knowledge, and wisdom infinitely greater than were ever shown by any of the children of men; and that He was indeed, what He claimed to be, and what by His mighty and merciful works He proved Himself to be,—the Son of the Living God, the Creator and Lord of all, coequal, coeternal with the Father [7].

5. This point being clear, let us also bear in mind,—as is evident from *external* testimony,—that the Old Testament existed in our Lord's age, precisely in the same condition as that in which it exists now. This has been already proved in the last discourse.

The entire Jewish Nation of that age *received the whole* of the Old Testament not as the Word of man, but as the Word of God. They guarded the sacred Text of the Old Testament with the most scrupulous fidelity and unremitting vigilance; they read the Old Testament publicly, Sabbath after Sabbath, throughout the year, in their Synagogues in almost all countries of the world; and, by reason of the

---

[7] John viii. 58; x. 30.

multiplication of copies of the Original and of Translations, that were requisite for this general public reading of the Old Testament in every clime, it was not possible for any one to tamper with the Text of the Old Testament, or to make any change in it, either by interpolation or mutilation.

6. Such was the state of things before Christ's coming, and at His coming into the world. And ever since that time, the Text of the Old Testament has been guarded by the twofold, independent, antagonistic custody of the Jewish Synagogue and of the Christian Church; so that we may confidently say, that the Old Testament which is now read in the Churches of England is the same as the Old Testament which was read in the Jewish Synagogues of our Lord's age. The Old Testament in *our* hands is precisely the same as the Old Testament which was in the hands of Jesus Christ.

7. Contemplate therefore Jesus Christ holding in His hands the Old Testament. How did *He* treat it? He Who proved by His wonderful deeds and words that He was far wiser than all the children of men, how did He treat the Old Testament? Did He treat it as "a common book?" Did He say that some parts of it are inspired, and other parts are not inspired? Did He say that some portions of it are genuine, and other portions are forged? Did He say that some of its contents are true, and that others are false?

The answer to these questions is easy. The Jews

guarded the Books of the Old Testament. They read these Books in their Synagogues every Sabbath, and they venerated all those Books,—they revered every part of those Books,—as true, as genuine, and as given by the inspiration of God[8].

To quote the words of their own writer, Josephus[9], it was "a principle innate in every Jew to regard those Books as oracles of God, and to cleave to them, yea, and to die gladly for them."

Now, how did our Blessed Lord treat this their national belief in the Inspiration of the Old Testament?

Did He censure the Jews for ascribing the Old Testament to God? Did He blame them for accepting every part of it as God's Word? If the Old Testament is merely the word of man, or if any portion of it is false, if any part of it is a forgery, Christ the Son of God would have blamed those who attributed it to God. He Who was so zealous of His Father's honour that He drove the buyers and sellers from the outer courts of His Father's House[1], would have rebuked those who ascribed the erring and illusory words of fallible and sinful man to the God of all Wisdom and Truth. The Son of God would have resented such an ascription; He would have de-

---

[8] It is altogether a false notion, that the Jews of our Lord's age regarded some Books of the Old Testament as possessing a higher degree of inspiration than others. The theory of *degrees* of inspiration is a fiction of a later date. Cp. Dr. W. Lee on Inspiration, Appendix C.

[9] See above, p. 38.

[1] Matt. xxi. 10. Mark xi. 15. Luke xix. 45. John ii. 15.

nounced such an imputation, as a profane outrage and insult against His awful majesty. He would not have connived at it. He would not have made Himself an accomplice with those who put forth counterfeit coin in the Name of the King of kings. He would not have abetted those who stamped that adulterated coinage with the Divine image and superscription, and circulated it throughout the world.

But hear what the Gospels relate of Christ.

Take, for instance, the chapter to which we have referred at the beginning of this discourse—the fourth chapter of St. Luke's Gospel. It begins with the history of the Temptation. There our Lord defeats the Tempter with the *sword of the Spirit, which is the Word of God*[2]. Thrice Satan assails Him, and thrice Christ foils him with this weapon, "It is written[3]." The Devil leaveth Him. Our Lord works miracles: and preaches in the Synagogues of Galilee. He comes to Nazareth. *As His custom was, He went into the Synagogue on the Sabbath Day. He there stood up to read.* In those Synagogues the Books of the Old Testament were *delivered to Him* as *the oracles of God*, and He received them as such. "To-day," He said, "is *this Scripture* fulfilled in your ears." On another occasion He said, *It is easier for heaven and earth to pass than one tittle of the Law to fail*[4]. Who then will venture to say that the Pentateuch is blemished with error? And again,

[2] Eph. vi. 14.   [3] Luke iv. 4. 8. 12.
[4] Luke xvi. 17. Cp. Matt. v. 18.

He declared that *the Scripture cannot be broken*[5]. Who then will assert that it is weak and fragile? The Son of God, when on earth, joined with the Jews, Sabbath after Sabbath, in their public worship; He took part with them in reading and expounding the Scriptures of the Old Testament as the inspired Word of God. Thus He declared that their belief in its Inspiration is true. He required all to receive it.

8. To give, if possible, greater solemnity to this divine declaration, Christ put it into the mouth of the Father of the faithful, Abraham, the Representative of all true Israelites; He utters it by the voice of Abraham, removed from this world, and dwelling in the blessed society of the spirits of the departed; of Moses, and David, and Isaiah, and all the Prophets. In the parable of Lazarus and the Rich Man, in which our Lord uplifts the veil which separates this world from the world of spirits, Christ reveals to us Abraham, and He makes Abraham speak that remarkable speech, *They have Moses and the Prophets, let them hear them. If they hear not Moses and the Prophets, neither will they be persuaded though one rose from the dead*[6]. Awfully solemn words, uttered by the Lord of Life, speaking by Abraham, the *Friend of God*.

They have Moses and the Prophets. Who therefore of us, that entertains a blessed hope that his own spirit may be carried by Angels at his own death into *Abraham's bosom*, and be there in peace with

---

[5] λυθῆναι, John x. 35. [6] Luke xvi. 29. 31.

those who have departed in the true faith and fear of God, will venture to deny that the Books which the Jews regarded as the Books of Moses and the Prophets, are not what they believed them to be,—true, genuine, and divine?

9. Yet more, after that the Son of God Himself had overcome Death, and when, on the evening of His glorious Resurrection, He walked with the two disciples to Emmaus, and when afterwards He appeared to His assembled Apostles, He appealed to the Books of the Old Testament as true, and as inspired by God; *Beginning at Moses and all the Prophets, He expounded to them in all the Scriptures the things concerning Himself*[7]. And He said, *These are the words which I spake unto you, that all things must be fulfilled which were written in the Law of Moses, and in the Prophets, and in the Psalms, concerning Me*[8].

Thus then our Lord and Saviour Jesus Christ has pronounced His divine verdict in behalf of the Truth, the Integrity, and Inspiration of the Old Testament. And this divine verdict, observe, applies to every part of the Old Testament. It covers the whole; it applies to every portion of all those Books which the Jews received as Holy Scripture.

The Son of God delivers to us the whole of the Old Testament, and commands all men to receive the whole as the Word of the Living God.

10. Accordingly we find that His Holy Apostles, being taught by Him, and by the Holy Spirit which

[7] Luke xxiv. 27.   [8] Luke xxiv. 44.

He sent down from heaven, declared that the Old Testament is inspired by God. Thus St. Peter speaks not only the opinion of his own Nation, but proclaims the judgment of Christ, when he says of the Hebrew Prophets, that their prophecy came *not by the will of man*, but that they spake what they spake, *being borne along by the Holy Ghost*[9]; and St. Paul reminds Timothy that the Scriptures which he had known from his childhood are *holy*, and are *the*[1] *writings which are able* to make him wise unto salvation through faith that is in Christ Jesus; and he adds that *every Scripture*—that is, every part of Scripture—is *given by inspiration of God*, or as the words signify, is *filled with the breath of God*[2].

IV. Here we may observe, in passing, that we have a ready answer for those who ask of us a reason, why we, of the Church of England, cannot agree with the Church of Rome in receiving the Apocrypha as inspired. We read some of the Apocrypha as useful and wholesome "for example of life and instruction of manners[3]," but we receive none of it *as inspired*. And thus we mark the essential difference that subsists between *all human writings*,—however excellent,

[9] 2 Pet. i. 21.
[1] τὰ δυνάμενα, observe the definitive Article, 2 Tim. iii. 15.
[2] The testimonies of the Ancient Fathers of the Church, in succession after the Apostles, witnesses to the Inspiration of the New Testament, as well as the Old, may be seen collected by Dr. Routh, Reliquiæ Sacræ, vol. v. pp. 336—353, and by the Rev. B. F. Westcott, Introduction to the Study of the Gospels, pp. 383—418.
[3] Thirty-nine Articles, Art. VI.

—and the *Holy Scriptures*, which are given by *inspiration of God*.

But the Church of Rome, at the Council of Trent in the sixteenth century (A.D. 1546), passed a decree affirming that the Apocryphal Books (such as Tobit, Judith, the Two Books of Maccabees) are of equal authority with the Books of Moses and the Prophets, and the rest of the Old Testament. She pronounced an anathema, or curse, on all who do not receive those Apocryphal Books as of equal authority with them.

What do we say to this? We say that those Apocryphal Books existed before the Son of God came down from heaven; and that they were never received by the Ancient Hebrew Church as inspired, and that they were never received as such by Jesus Christ. We receive the Old Testament,—neither more nor less,—which was received by Jesus Christ. Therefore the words of Rome, directed against *us*, are words spoken against Christ. We care not therefore for her anathemas, except for her sake. For we know from St. Paul, that *no man speaking by the Spirit of God calleth Jesus accursed* [4]; and that our love for Christ is to be shown by hearkening to His Word; and that *Whosoever loveth not the Lord Jesus Christ*, says the same Apostle, *let him be anathema* [5].

V. Let us now apply these things to ourselves and to the circumstances of our own times.

---

[4] 1 Cor. xii. 3.   [5] 1 Cor. xvi. 22.

1. Is the Old Testament true? Is it from heaven? Is it all true? Is it all inspired? These questions are now current among us. Books are put into our hands, written, it would seem, by shrewd men, distinguished by literary attainments, and by philosophic calmness and research, who appear to have inquired with candour and impartiality into the evidences of the Truth and Inspiration of the Old Testament, and *not* to have been convinced that it is of divine origin. We hear it alleged by some, that it can be shown from recent investigations of Geologists, that the world must have existed *before* the date assigned to the creation by the Book of Genesis. We hear it argued by others, who seem to be proficients in the study of Morals and Metaphysics, that to believe all mankind to have been involved in guilt by the sin of Adam and Eve, is hardly consistent with the reverence due to the Justice and Benevolence of God: and that it is derogatory to His Wisdom and Foresight, to suppose that He should have destroyed His own work of Creation by the general devastation of the Flood.

What, they ask, are we to say of such seemingly strange and incredible narratives as those which are found in the Old Testament, concerning the speaking of Balaam's ass, and the coming forth of the Prophet Jonah from the whale's belly after three days? What are we to think of these things?

Again, it is said by some persons of high reputation among us, reviving the sceptical objections of

Porphyry[6] which were exploded by S. Jerome[7] fourteen hundred years ago, that the prophecies of Daniel[8] bear marks of having been composed after the events which they profess to foretell,—and, in fact, are no prophecies at all.

2. To those who may make these, and all such allegations as these, impugning the Truth, Genuineness, or Inspiration of the Old Testament, we would put this question,—Whom shall we believe,—you, or JESUS CHRIST?

You allege, that there are certain things in the Old Testament, which you cannot reconcile with the results of your physical researches, or with your moral and metaphysical theories; and you therefore reject the Old Testament, and require us to surrender it in deference to your authority.

But in this great question—in this most momentous question of eternal life or eternal death—we ask again, *Whom* shall we believe, *whom* shall we follow? You, or JESUS CHRIST? Shall we imagine that you, the creatures of a day, have a clearer insight into the Laws of Nature, than He who made the worlds[9], and who controlled the Laws of Nature by the utterance of a single word? Shall we suppose

---

[6] And of some Jews *since our Lord's age*, who perceive that the Messiah must be come, if Daniel is a Prophet. See Hottinger, Thesaur. Philol. p. 504.

[7] See S. Jerome, Præfat. in Danielem, tom. iii. p. 1071, ed. Benedict. Paris, 1704.

[8] "Essays and Reviews," pp. 69. 76.

[9] John i. 3. Heb. i. 2.

that you have more knowledge of the history and structure of the Universe, than He who swayed the Elements, and walked on the Sea, and calmed the Storm, and made the Earth give up her dead, and mounted on the clouds of Heaven? Shall we listen to those metaphysical theorists, who would have us give up the Old Testament, which was received as a Divine Book by Him who read the heart, and knew what was in man, and foretold things to come? Shall we give credence to those Moralists, who reject the Old Testament, which was acknowledged to be God's Word by that Divine Teacher of Moral Virtue who preached the Sermon on the Mount; and whose Religion, wherever it has been received, has emancipated the Slave, and beautified Marriage, and has given a grace and dignity to Woman, which she never before possessed since she was Eve in Paradise, and has opened a pure well-spring of blessing and of joy in every Christian family, and prepares its members, by the discipline of love on earth, for the life of angels in heaven?

In what appertains to the Word of God let us not pretend to be wiser than the Son of God. Let us not reject a single iota of the Old Testament, with frail and fallible children of men, but reverently receive the whole with the Son of God.

He has delivered to us the Old Testament: He who is now enthroned in glory, commands us to receive it. Alas! for those who *refuse Him that speaketh from heaven*[1]. For He has warned us that he that *believeth and is baptized shall be saved, and he who believeth not shall be damned*[2]. Inexpressibly awful words, uttered by the Judge of all, who hath *the Keys of Hell and Death*[3]. He will one day be revealed *in flaming fire taking vengeance on them that obey not the Gospel*[4]. And then it will be seen by all, and it will be felt by the children of darkness, that while He is infinite in mercy to all who believe and obey Him, yet to all who do not believe Him, *our God is a consuming fire*[5].

3. Looking, then, to Christ holding the New Testament in His hands, we are not staggered by any difficulties in it. We expect to find some difficulties in a Revelation from a Being like God to such a creature as man. We even rejoice in these difficulties. We do not fear them as enemies, but welcome them as allies, and embrace them as friends; for they are occasions of our growth in grace. They exercise our humility. They are the leaves and flowers, of which our heavenly crown is woven. They remind us of our own weakness and ignorance, and of the power and wisdom of Christ. They send us to Him, and to the Gospel. They make us to go and sit down as little children at the feet of Jesus Christ.

4. Thus, for instance, the *history of Balaam*. It may be a difficulty to some. But it will remind

---

[1] Heb. xii. 25.   [2] Mark xiv. 16.   [3] Rev. i. 18.
[4] 2 Thess. i. 7.   [5] Heb. xii. 29.

every Christian reader, who really loves his Saviour, that the Apostle of Christ, St. Peter, who was enabled by Christ to heal the sick, and raise the dead, and to speak with tongues [6], and to discern the spirits, as in the case of Ananias [7], and to foretell the future, has referred to the history of Balaam in the second chapter of his second Epistle. The Apostle St. Peter accepts the history of Balaam, and does not rationalize it away, but explains its inner meaning, and reminds us how by that signal example, God showed, that even the most despised of the brute creatures themselves are wiser and more clear-sighted than a disobedient Prophet, or a sceptical Philosopher. *The dumb ass speaking with man's voice*, says the Apostle, *forbad the madness of the Prophet* [8].

5. Thus again as to the *history of Jonah in the whale's belly*. It may be a difficulty with some; but in reading that history every Christian student, who believes and adores his Blessed Redeemer, will recollect, that Jesus Christ has adopted and authenticated that history, and has applied and appropriated it to Himself. *As Jonas was three days and three nights in the whale's belly, so* (says Christ) *shall the Son of Man be three days and three nights in the heart of the earth* [9]. The Christian reader will observe, that Christ's reference to the history of Jonah is interwoven with Christ's prophecy concerning Himself; and he will

---

[6] Acts ii. 4; iii. 7; ix. 34. 40.   [7] Acts v. 3.
[8] 2 Pet. ii. 16.   [9] Matt. xii. 40.

remember that Christ's word was proved to be true by the fulfilment of that prophecy. Christ *was* three days and three nights in the heart of the earth; and He then raised Himself. Thus Christ's authorization of Jonah's history is verified by the fulfilment of Christ's prophecy concerning Himself, of Whom Jonah was a type. Let us not read the history of Jonah by the feeble glimmerings of a purblind sciolism, but by the clear light of Christ's glorious Gospel, and we shall see the proof of its truth in His burial and resurrection. Thus these Scriptural difficulties are dissolved by a spiritual alchymy in the crucible of faith.

6. Once more: the unbeliever may allege that the prophecies of *Daniel* correspond so minutely with the events that they profess to predict that they must be posterior to those events. A strange allegation! As if there were any past or future with God! As if He, who spake by the Prophets, does not see all things present at once. It is enough for us to know that the Book of Daniel, as it is in our hands now, was in the hands of the Jewish nation of our Lord's age; and was received by them as inspired [1]; and that what they received as inspired was also received as such by Jesus Christ. Indeed

---

[1] See the remarkable testimony of the Jewish historian Josephus, Antiquities, book x. chapters 10—12. See also Maimonides, More Nevochim, ii. 45, who says, "*Daniel*, the Psalms, &c., are all written by the *Holy Spirit.*" How different is this language, and that of Christ, from the language of " Essays and Reviews," where it is said (p. 77) that " the *current error*," as to the Book of Daniel, "is discreditable " to divines.

He expressly owns Daniel as a prophet. "When ye shall see the abomination of desolation, spoken of by *Daniel the Prophet*[2]."—Daniel the Prophet may be no Prophet to the unbeliever; the book of Daniel may be a forgery to the sceptic of the nineteenth century; but to us, my Christian friends, let him be Daniel the Prophet; for he *was* Daniel the Prophet to his own nation, he was Daniel the Prophet to Jesus Christ.

VI. Let us here acknowledge our own spiritual privileges, and our cause for thankfulness to God. The Jews of old were greatly favoured by Him, but how much more favoured are we! "What advantage hath the *Jew?*" asks the Apostle. "Much every way," he replies, "chiefly because unto them were committed the oracles of God." And may we not much more say, "What advantage hath the *Christian?* Much every way;" even more than the Jew. For *we* have a stronger assurance of the Divine Inspiration of the Hebrew Scriptures than even the Hebrews themselves had. They received the Old Testament as inspired, on the testimony of their forefathers, but it is delivered to us, as inspired, by Jesus Christ Himself. Here is an inexpressible comfort; here indeed is a joyful assurance, in days like these, of rebuke and blasphemy. Here we have hope and peace in the sorrows of life, and in the hour of death. *Our* belief in the Truth and Inspiration of

---

[2] Matt. xxiv. 15. Mark xiii. 14. Dan. ix. 27; xii. 11.

the Old Testament, yes, of the *whole* of the Old Testament, rests on a foundation that can never be shaken. It rests on the testimony of Christ. Therefore we may dwell safely, and defy the storms raging around us. Let the rain descend; let the floods of Unbelief come, and the winds of false Doctrine blow, and beat upon our house; it will *not* fall, for it *is built upon a Rock*[3]. It is built upon the *Rock of Ages*[4]; it is built upon Jesus Christ.

VII. Finally, may we not say, that the written Word of God is like the Incarnate Word Himself,— *set for the fall, and also for the rising of many in Israel, and for a sign that shall be spoken against*[5]?

Holy Scripture is set for our moral probation, which supposes trial and difficulty. It exhibits us to men and angels as we are. It displays what *manner of spirit we are of*[6]. It proves, whether we have those moral habits and tempers of mind, and those dispositions of meekness and docility, and readiness to weigh evidence with candour and fairness, without which no man is *fit for the kingdom of God*[7].

Holy Scripture is set for our *fall*,—if, with a partial eye to difficulties in single texts taken by themselves, and without due regard to the general scope of the whole, and to the evidence of its Truth and Inspiration, we take occasion to cavil at its contents, and deny its divine origin and authority.

But, on the other hand, thanks be to God, it is

---

[3] Matt. vii. 24, 25.   [4] Isa. xxvi. 4.   [5] Luke ii. 34.
[6] Luke ix. 55.   [7] Luke ix. 62.

Those difficulties will be cleared away from the eyes of those who use them aright.

also set for our *rising*,—for our rising to heavenly glory,—if we use those difficulties aright; and are led thereby to acknowledge the weakness of our own faculties in their present state, and our consequent need of divine grace; and to exercise humility, and to thank God for what is *perfectly clear* in Holy Scripture; and to look forward with faith and hope to that blessed time, when all those difficulties will be dispersed, and the film and mist, which now cloud our spiritual vision, will be purged away; and we shall no longer see, as now, *through a glass darkly*, but shall *see face to face*, and *know even as we are known* [3].

[3] 1 Cor. xiii. 12.

LECTURE IV.

Luke xi. 33.

No man, when he hath lighted a candle, putteth it in a secret place, neither under a bushel, but on a candlestick, that they which come in may see the light [1].

WE have been engaged in considering, what the reasons are for belief in the Inspiration of the *Old* Testament.

I. The subject now proposed for examination is;—
On what grounds do we receive the *New* Testament as the Inspired Word of God?

1. God is One, and Everlasting; and *if* the *New* Testament is from Him, we may reasonably anticipate, that the method employed by Him for assuring us of the Inspiration of the *New* Testament, will, as far as the difference of circumstances allows, be similar to that plan by which He has assured us of the Inspiration of the Old.

2. When we were asked for the reasons of our belief in the Inspiration of the *Old* Testament, our answer was,—

---

[1] Cp. Matt. v. 15. Mark iv. 21. Luke viii. 16.

First, we receive the Old Testament on the authority of God Himself, speaking by the universal consent and practice of the Hebrew Nation, to which, as the Apostle says, *were committed the Oracles of God*[2].

Next we proceeded to show, that when the Son of God Himself came down from heaven, and dwelt among us, He acknowledged the truth of that belief in the Inspiration of the Old Testament. Our Blessed Lord declared His own concurrence in, and pronounced His divine approval of, this consent and practice of the Hebrew Nation, receiving all the Books of the Old Testament, as set apart from all other Volumes then existing in the world, and as holy and divine Writings, dictated by the Spirit of God.

Therefore we affirm, that the Old Testament comes to us ministerially and instrumentally *through* the ancient Jewish Church; but it comes to us effectually and virtually *from* the hands of JESUS CHRIST.

3. Our present assertion is, that Almighty God has employed similar means for assuring us of the Inspiration of the *New* Testament.

We affirm that the New Testament comes to us,—*through* the instrumentality of the Christian Church,—its divinely appointed Guardian and Keeper,—but it comes to us principally and originally from JESUS CHRIST.

We look up to heaven with the eye of Faith, and

[2] Rom. iii. 1, 2.

we see JESUS CHRIST, the Incarnate WORD, enthroned there in His glorious Majesty, and holding in His hands the Old and New Testaments, and delivering to us both Testaments, as the Word of the Living God.

4. In order to show the soundness of this belief, we must revert to a proposition already proved in a previous discourse, namely, that the *Four Gospels* are *true*³.

That the *Four Gospels* are *true*, has been shown from the facts, that the Gospels were publicly *read* in Christian Churches in primitive times; and that they who read them could not have been deceived as to their veracity; and that they died gladly in defence of their truth: and that eventually the Roman Empire, which had at first persecuted the Christians for belief in the Gospels, was itself converted to Christianity, and received the Gospels as *true*.

II. The *truth* of the Gospels being established, it follows that the Son of God uttered those sayings which He is related in the Gospels to have spoken.

1. Among the declarations of Christ recorded in the Gospels, we find the following: *Upon this Rock I will build My Church, and the gates of hell shall not prevail against it*⁴. *Lo, I am with you alway, even unto the end of the world*⁵. Christ promised to send the Holy Spirit to His disciples, to *lead them into all*

See above, pp. 56—59.   ⁴ Matt. xvi. 18.   ⁵ Matt. xxviii. 20.

truth, *and to abide with them for ever. These things have I spoken unto you, being yet present with you; but the Comforter, which is the Holy Ghost, whom the Father will send in My name, He shall teach you all things, and bring all things to your remembrance, whatsoever I have said unto you*[6]. And, *When He, the Spirit of Truth, is come, He will guide you into all truth: for He shall not speak of Himself; but whatsoever He shall hear, that shall He speak, and He will show you things to come*[7]. *I will pray the Father, and He will give you another Comforter, that He may abide with you for ever, even the Spirit of Truth*[8]. And again, *I will give you a mouth and wisdom, which all your adversaries shall not be able to gainsay nor resist*[9].

The fulfilment of these promises of Christ is avouched in the history of the Acts of the Apostles[1], the truth of which is proved by its reception and public reading in the primitive Churches of Christendom.

2. Hence we may conclude, that Christ enabled His Apostles and Evangelists to reveal supernatural mysteries; and that the words which they have delivered to the Church for her perpetual instruction in divine truth, and which have been read as such in her public assemblies from their age until now, are *not* words which *man's wisdom teacheth, but which the Holy Ghost teacheth*[2].

---

[6] John xiv. 25, 26.
[8] John xiv. 16.
[1] Acts ii. 4.
[7] John xvi. 13.
[9] Luke xxi. 15.
[2] 1 Cor. ii. 13.

and He instituted the Church as a Witness of the Inspiration of the Scriptures written by them.

3. Next, we may deduce from Christ's words just rehearsed, this inference—that He has instituted in the world a visible Society, called His Church, to which He has promised His perpetual presence and His Spirit, to lead it into all truth, and to abide with it unto the end.

Accordingly, we find that the Apostle St. Paul, having regard to Christ's promise of His continual presence in His Church, calls her His *Body;* and meditating on His love to His Church, and her dearness to Him, he speaks of her as united to Christ in spiritual wedlock[3]; and forasmuch as she is quickened, informed, and taught by Christ's Spirit dwelling in her, and publishing by her, as by a living organ, His will and word, the Apostle says, that she *is the Church of the Living God, the Pillar and Ground of the Truth*[4].

We cannot say with some persons, that we receive the Scriptures as divine because *we* know *who* their writers were, and that they were good men full of the Holy Ghost, and that *therefore* whatever they wrote must be inspired of God.

The truth is, we do *not* know, by *whom* some of the Books of Scripture were written[5]; and this

---

[3] Eph. v. 23—32. [4] 1 Tim. iii. 15.
[5] E. g. the Books of Job, Judges, and others in the Old Testament. The Epistle to the Hebrews in the New Testament was, in all *probability*, written by St. Paul; but its *inspiration* is not only probable, but *certain:* because it is received, as inspired, by the Universal Church of God.

Besides, the *authorship* of some smaller portions of the Gospels may

uncertainty seems to have been intended to serve a providential purpose, in order that we might not attribute the authority of the Scriptures to the *men* by whose instrumentality they were written, but to God who wrote the Scriptures by their hands.

We receive the Books of Holy Scripture on the testimony of Christ, speaking in His Church.

III. One of the principal offices of the Church of God, ever since Scripture was written, has been to guard Scripture, and to read it openly and habitually to the people, and to authenticate it as God's Word[6].

1. We find, that as soon as the first Books of Scripture—namely, the Books of Moses—were written, they were deposited by God's command for safe custody, near the Ark, in the Holy of Holies; and that they were ordered to be read publicly at the Feast of Tabernacles as His Holy Word[7].

These commands of God were the first beginnings of a great and comprehensive Plan for the safe preservation of the Holy Scriptures, and for their publication to the world, and for the attestation of their divine origin and authority.

The ancient Hebrew Church read the Old Testament in the Synagogues, Sabbath after Sabbath, year after year, and century after century, in all parts of

---

be matter of doubt: and this very circumstance brings out more clearly the grounds on which our belief in their Inspiration rests. The author may here be allowed to refer to his notes on Mark xvi. 9—20, and on John vii. 53; viii. 1—11.

[6] Cp. Hooker, V. xxii. 2.   [7] See above, pp. 43—45.

the world. It read the Old Testament as inspired by God.

When the Son of God Himself came down from heaven, He took part, as we have already seen [8], in this public reading of the Old Testament in the Hebrew Synagogues; He acknowledged the Old Testament, which was there read, to be what the ancient Hebrew Church believed and testified it to be,—the unerring Word of God.

2. This providential arrangement for the guardianship and authentication of God's Word, by means of public Reading, was maintained and enlarged, from the time of the writing of the first Books of the *Old Testament* until Christ's First Advent; and ever since that time it has been growing and expanding itself throughout the world by the planting and propagation of Christian Churches in distant lands; and it will continue to extend itself by the preaching of *the Gospel as a witness unto all Nations even unto the end* [9], when Christ will come again to judge the World.

3. This divinely-instituted plan of public Reading comprehends within its range the *New* Testament, as well as the Old; and places the *New* Testament on the same footing with the Old.

This will appear from the history of the publication and preservation of the New Testament.

4. One of the most remarkable portions of the

---

[8] See above pp. 61—65.   [9] Matt. xxiv. 14.

New Testament in this particular respect, is that which we have been reading in the Church during the last week, namely, the First and Second Epistles of St. Paul to the Church of Thessalonica.

These two Epistles were the first written of all St. Paul's Epistles, and were among the first written of all the Books of the New Testament.

It is observable, that in the first of these two Epistles to the Thessalonians, St. Paul gives a solemn injunction, as follows: *I charge,* or adjure *you, by the Lord, that this Epistle be read unto all the holy brethren* [10]. *That* Epistle was to be *read openly* in the Church. And in another Epistle,—that to the Colossians,—St Paul takes for granted that it would be *read* in the Church. He thus speaks: *When this Epistle is read among you, cause that it be read also in the Church of the Laodiceans* [1].

What St. Paul required to be done to his own Epistles, was done to *all* the Books of the New Testament. They were *received* and *read openly* and habitually on every Lord's Day, year after year and century after century, in Christian Churches, from primitive times [2].

5. And with what feelings were they received and read? Were they regarded as *common* writings? No: certainly not. They were received and read as the *Word of God.* They were reverently received as such; they were received and read as *Holy Scrip-*

---

[10] 1 Thess. v. 27.   [1] Col. iv. 16.   [2] See above, pp. 82, 83.

ture[3]; they were read simultaneously with the Books of the *Old* Testament. They were read as *equally inspired* with the Books of *Moses* and the *Prophets*[4], which had been received by Jesus Christ Himself, as the Word of the Living God.

Thus the Church of God bore witness to them, and testified that they are the Oracles of God[5].

6. Let us also consider this. The writers of the New Testament lay claim to Inspiration. Thus St. Paul says to the Corinthians, *I trow*[6] *that I have the Spirit of God*[7]. And, *We speak not in words which man's wisdom teacheth, but which the Holy Ghost teacheth*[8]. And he appeals to his miracles wrought among them in proof of his Inspiration. *Truly the signs of an Apostle were wrought among you in all patience, in signs, and wonders, and mighty deeds*[9].

The Epistles of St. Paul, in which these words occur, contain severe reprehensions of those to whom these Epistles were sent. He reproves them as *carnal*, as *babes in Christ*, and yet *puffed up*[1]. Those persons were proud of their intellectual and spiritual gifts;

---

[3] It is remarkable that the word Γραφὴ, which simply means *writing*, is reserved and appropriated in the New Testament (where it occurs fifty times) to the *sacred* writings, i.e. to the *Holy Scriptures;* and marks the separation of the *Scriptures* from all "common books," indeed, from *all other writings* in the world.

[4] See Bingham, Antiquities, XIV. ch. iii.

[5] Cp. Hooker, V. xxii. 2: "The reading of the Word of God in open audience is the plainest evidence we have of the Church's assent and acknowledgment that it *is* His Word."

[6] δοκῶ.
[7] 1 Cor. vii. 40.
[8] 1 Cor. ii. 13.
[9] 2 Cor. xii. 12.
[1] 1 Cor. iii. 1—3; v. 2.

and the *reception* of those Epistles involved a censure on themselves; and they would never have received those Epistles as inspired, unless they had been convinced, that the claims of the writer to Inspiration were true.

The reception of *all* the Books of the New Testament as of equally divine authority, is a proof of their Inspiration.

IV. But it may be asked,—

Are there not *some portions* of the *New Testament* which were *not* at first received universally as the inspired Word of God?

Yes, certainly there are.

The whole primitive Church received the Four Gospels, and the Acts of the Apostles, the Thirteen Epistles which bear the name of St. Paul, and the First Epistle of St. Peter and of St. John. These Books were universally received at once by all Christendom.

But some *few minor parts* of the New Testament there are, concerning which some particular Churches at first suspended their judgment.

Such, for instance, was the Second Epistle of St. Peter.

Some Churches waited for a time, and did not pronounce judgment upon that Epistle, till they were fully persuaded of its genuineness and inspiration. But, after careful examination, they received it; and eventually *all* Churches in Christendom received *all* the Books of the New Testament as the Word of God.

Inferences to be derived from the partial non-reception, 87
and subsequent universal reception, of those portions.

This very fact, that *some* of the Books of the New Testament were *not* received at first, is of great value. For it proves the scrupulous care, with which those Books were *examined*, before they were received by the Church; and the fact also, that those Books, concerning which some Churches doubted at first, were at length received by *all* Churches, proves that they were rightly received.

V. To this testimony of the Catholic Church of God, receiving and reading the whole of the New Testament, we appeal in support of our own belief that all and every part of it is the Word of God.

1. Let us here obviate an objection.

Let no one imagine, that in speaking of the *Catholic* Church we mean the *Church of Rome;* or that in appealing to the testimony of the Church *Catholic* in this matter, we are appealing to the testimony of the *Roman* Church. No. The Roman Church is not the Catholic Church. The Church of Rome is a part, but, in many respects, a very unsound part, of the Catholic Church.

In her Canon of the *Old* Testament, she displays her own unsoundness, by receiving as inspired the Apocrypha [2]; which was never received as such by the Ancient Hebrew Church, nor by Jesus Christ, the Head of the Universal Church, nor by His Holy Apostles, nor by the Catholic Church [3].

With regard to the New Testament, we receive as

---

[2] See above, pp. 66, 67.
[3] As is proved by Bp. Cosin in his Scholastical History of the

inspired Scripture the same Books as the Church of Rome does. It is true there is no difference between her and us on this point. Happily, the difference is limited to the Books of the *Old* Testament; and there Christ Himself decides the controversy by His own direct testimony. And we rest on that.

As to the New Testament, we receive the same Books as the Church of Rome does; but we do *not* receive them on *her* authority. We receive them on the authority of Christ, speaking to us by the Catholic, or Universal, Church.

2. Again; let it not be supposed, that we are of opinion with some in the Church of Rome[4], that the *Church* can *give authority* to *Scripture*. No; the authority of Scripture comes from God, and God alone. The light is not from the Candlestick, but from the Candles; it is not from the Church, but from the Scriptures, which are the Candles that Christ has lighted, and set in the Church. But the Church *testifies* to the divine authority of Scripture. John the Baptist was a *shining light*[5], and bore *witness* to Christ. That witness was true; for John was *full of the Holy Ghost*[6] Who spake by him. But John did not *give* any authority to Christ. So the Church bears testimony to Scripture, and we

---

Canon of the Scripture, Lond. 1657, 1672, 1683; or in vol. iii. of his Works, Oxford, 1849.

[4] Whose assertions to this effect may be seen in the Author's volume on the Canon of Scripture, p. 15.

[5] John v. 35.   Luke i. 15.

appeal to *that* testimony as true: we appeal to it as the testimony of Christ, and of the Holy Ghost.

And why? Because Christ has said, *that the gates of hell shall never prevail against His Church*[7], and *that He will be ever with her, and will send her the Holy Spirit to guide her into all truth, and to abide with her for ever*[8].

If the New Testament, which the Universal Church receives and reads as the Word of God, is only the word of *man*; *if* the Church of God has *not* been led into truth in this vital matter; *if* the whole Church of Christ has fallen into error in this fundamental article concerning the Inspiration of the New Testament, on which the fabric of her faith, and hope, and charity is built, then—we say it with all reverence—Christ's promise to His Church has failed. He has *not* sent the Holy Spirit to lead her into all truth.

But, God forbid, my brethren, that any one should imagine this!

Christ is the Truth. He is the everlasting *Yea* and *Amen*[9]. *Heaven and earth will pass away, but His word will not pass away*[10]. Therefore His promise of presence and guidance to His Church has *not* failed. He speaks to us by her, to whom He has sent His Spirit, and He assures us by her voice and practice that *all* the Books of the New Testament, which she reads as inspired, were given by the inspiration of God.

[7] Matt. xvi. 18.
[8] John xiv. 16; xvi. 13.
[9] Rev. iii. 14. Cp. 2 Cor. i. 20.
[10] Luke xxi. 33.

VI. Thanks be to God, the Church of England was endued with wisdom, at her Reformation in the sixteenth century, to build her belief, and her people's belief, in the Inspiration of Holy Scripture, on this good foundation.

1. *She* did *not* say,—what some *other* religious communities *did* say at that time [1],—that men's belief in the Inspiration of Scripture is to rest on their own inner illumination, or personal consciousness. She did not build her house on such a floating quicksand as that. No: she appealed to the public judgment and concurrent practice of the Church of Christ Universal. In her Sixth Article [2] she says, in words worthy to be written in letters of gold in every church of the British Empire, " In the name of the HOLY SCRIPTURE we do understand those Canonical Books of the OLD and NEW TESTAMENT, of whose authority was never any *doubt in the Church.*" And because she well knew that there are *some few portions* of the *New* Testament—such as the Second Epistle of St. Peter, as already stated—concerning which there *were some doubts* at first in *some* Churches, but which were afterwards universally received, without any doubt, by the *whole Catholic Church*, she wisely adds, at the close of the same Article: "All the Books of the *New* Testament, *as they are commonly*

---

[1] See above, p. 23.
[2] Thirty-nine Articles of the Church of England " as agreed upon by the Archbishops and Bishops of both Provinces and the whole Clergy, in the Convocation holden at London in the year 1562."

received, we do receive and account them canonical."

She also shows, *what* those Books are, by her Authorized Version of the Bible, and by her Calendar of Lessons of Holy Scripture, appointed to be read daily throughout the year.

2. We cannot be too thankful, that the Church of our beloved Country was mercifully preserved from building on an unsound foundation in this most momentous matter. Three centuries have elapsed since that Article was published; and every year that passes, bears witness to the wisdom with which it was framed.

We have seen, and now see, that other religious Communities—particularly those foreign Protestant Churches,—which did *not* build on this foundation, but on the loose and sandy substruction of private opinion, or personal feeling, in this great question of Inspiration—have been, and are now, buffeted and bewildered by the winds and storms of Infidelity. They have separated Holy Scripture from the Church, which is the appointed Keeper and Guardian of Scripture; and therefore they have almost forfeited Scripture. There is scarcely any portion of the Bible, which has not now been gainsaid and rejected by some of their most eminent Teachers, relying with fond and overweening conceit on their own private imaginations; and dogmatizing rashly and recklessly on God's Holy Word, with arbitrary wilfulness, proud presumption, fickle caprice, and disdainful contempt of authority. They declaim loudly against the Roman Papacy, but every one among them sets up a private Popedom in his own person, and claims spiritual infallibility and supremacy for himself, and lords it over the faith of men. This opinionative dictation of crude, ill-digested opinions has engendered endless strife; this irrational abuse of reason, and injudicious perversion of private judgment, have brought discredit upon Reason, and have been disastrous to Faith.

3. Blessed be God, the Church of England has not been led astray by this fanatical spirit. Blessed be God, she has been enabled to discharge faithfully the duty of a Church in the public reading of Holy Writ. Blessed be God, she reads day by day, throughout the year, several chapters of Holy Scripture to the People in their mother tongue. Blessed also be God, she builds her belief in the Inspiration of Scripture on a sound foundation; she builds it on the testimony of Christ, speaking by His Church to the world.

4. This method of proof has been dictated by Christ Himself. *No man,* He says, *when he hath lighted a candle, putteth it in a secret place, neither under a bushel, but on a Candlestick, that they which come in may see the light.* And again He said, *No man lighteth a candle and covereth it with a vessel, or putteth it under a bed; but setteth it on a Candlestick, that they which enter in may see the light.*

in which the Candles of Scripture are lighted and set by Christ, the Light of the World.

Christ is the *Light of the World*[3]. He lighted the candles of Holy Scripture, and He has put them into the Candlestick of His Church, which is appointed to guard and bear the light of Scripture which is kindled by Christ. Therefore Christ Himself, in the Book of Revelation, describes a *Church* under the figure of a *Candlestick*[4].

Observe those seven-branched Candlesticks standing before the Altar of this Church. They are now dark. And why? Because they have no candles in them. Such is a Church without Scripture. It is dark; a Candlestick without light. But put the Candles of Scripture into the Candlestick of the Church, and all will see the light.

Again, if you light the candles, but put them into the vault or crypt[5]; or if you strew them on the ground, the candles are of little use; they soon go out. So, if you bury the Bible in the crypt and vault of a dead language, it is of little use. If you hide it from the people, it is of little use. Or if you smother it with the bushel of secular business, or put it beneath the bed of carnal indulgence, it is of little use.

Or if, on the other hand, you scatter Bibles about

---

[3] John viii. 12; ix. 5.

[4] λυχνία—properly a *lamp-stand*; a term even more significant of this office of the Church, than the English word *candlestick*: for the Lamp is fed with *oil*, which is an appropriate emblem of Holy Scripture, bestowed by the Holy Spirit, the Giver of Divine unction and grace, illuminating the world. See Rev. i. 11—13.

[5] κρύπτην, the true reading in the text, Luke xi. 33.

at random, and do not put them into the Candlestick of the Church, they will be puffed and blown about with every wind of doctrine, and will flare and smoke, and soon go out.

You must have the Candles, and you must have the Candlestick; and you must put the Candles into the Candlestick, and they will give light to all.

Christ has lighted the Candles of Holy Scripture, and He has set them in the Candlestick of His Church. Let us not separate the Candles from the Candlestick, lest we derive no profit from either. Let us not sever the Bible from the Church, lest we lose both.

5. Look up to heaven. Behold Christ. *He is the true Light that lighteth every man that cometh into the world*[6]. He enlightened Moses, He enlightened the Prophets before His Incarnation, He enlightened the Apostles and Evangelists after His Incarnation. He sent the Holy Ghost to *teach them all things, and to guide them into all truth, and to bring to their remembrance whatsoever He had said unto them*, and to fill up the light of the Holy Scriptures *which are able to make us wise unto salvation through faith in Him*[7].

Christ, the Everlasting Word, is the Author and Giver of the written Word[8].

6. Further, Christ is the Truth. He is *the Way,*

---

[6] John i. 9.   [7] 2 Tim. iii. 15.

[8] S. Augustine de Consens. Evangel. lib. i. cap. ult. well says, "Qui Prophetas *ante* Suam descensionem misit, Ipse et Apostolos post Suam ascensionem misit . . . quicquid Ille de Suis factis et dictis nos legere voluit, hoc scribendum illis tanquam Suis manibus imperavit."

the Truth, and the Life[9]. He *is the faithful and true Witness*[1]. He not only gave the Scriptures, but He bears testimony to their Inspiration. When He came down from Heaven and took our flesh, He acknowledged all the Books of the Old Testament to be given by Inspiration of God. And after His ascension into heaven, He established His Church, and sent His Holy Spirit to be for ever with her; and He speaks in her, and by her, and He declares by her voice and practice, that the Scriptures of the New Testament, no less than the Old, are the Word of the Living God.

VII. Lastly, Christ gives the Holy Spirit to all those who seek for Him aright. He punishes ungodly men with spiritual blindness, so that they cannot see the light blazing forth in Holy Scripture. He chastises those who lead unholy lives; who would quench the light of Scripture, if they could, for it speaks to them of a Judgment to come. He allows them to close their eyes, and leaves them to themselves. Infidelity is the punishment which evil men inflict on themselves by their sins. *Every one that doeth evil hateth the light, neither cometh to the light, lest his deeds should be reproved*[2]. Nor is it only carnal indulgence, or worldliness, which produce spiritual blindness. Spiritual blindness often co-exists with great mental endowments. It is engendered by intellectual pride. God hides Himself *from the wise*

---

[9] John xiv. 6.   [1] Rev. iii. 14.   [2] John iii. 20.

and prudent, but revealeth Himself unto babes³. He resisteth the proud, but giveth grace unto the humble⁴. The angels of Christ's little ones see the face of God⁵. We must become as little children, if we would behold Him, and see the *wondrous things of His Law*⁶. In order that the mind may be clear, the heart must be clean. We must seek for the truth not by wrangling disputations, but by loving thoughts and words and deeds, by lowly reverence on our knees. We must seek it by holiness of life. *If any man does God's will,* He will make him *know of the doctrine*⁷. If any man *love God, the same is known of God*⁸, and is loved of God, and God reveals Himself to him. *Mysteries are revealed unto the meek*⁹. *Them that are meek shall He guide in judgment; and such as are gentle, them shall He learn His way*¹.

Is this temper yours? Are these dispositions yours? Then, God knows, you will be enchanted and enraptured with the beauty and loveliness of Holy Scripture; you will be transported with holy ecstasy in hearing and reading it. It will sound in your ears like heavenly music, chanted by the quires of the Seraphim. By the aid of the Holy Spirit *shed abroad in your hearts,* in answer to your prayers, you will see the work of the Spirit in the Bible. You will say, *Lord, how I love Thy Law, all the day*

---

³ Luke x. 21.   ⁴ James iv. 6. 1 Pet. v. 5.
⁵ Matt. xviii. 10.   ⁶ Ps. cxix. 18.
⁷ John vii. 17.   ⁸ 1 Cor. viii. 3.
⁹ Ecclus. iii. 19.   ¹ Ps. xxv. 8.

*long is my study in it. I rejoice at Thy Word as one that findeth great spoil*². *Thy testimonies are my delight and my counsellors*³. *More to be desired are they than gold, yea, than much fine gold, sweeter also than honey and the honeycomb*⁴. You will never be weary of admiring the harmonious symmetry of all the parts of the Bible, the unsullied holiness of its precepts, the exact fulfilment of its prophecies, the tender graciousness of its promises, the marvellous glory of its revelations, displaying Christ the *Sun of Righteousness,* illumining our dark nature with the brilliant splendour of His light, and dwelling therein with the Shechinah of His Presence, and pouring upon it the riches of His grace, and preparing it for the everlasting fruition of heavenly bliss. You will never be tired of meditating on the wonderful adaptation of the Scriptures to our nature and our needs, to our cares and our sorrows, to our fears and our hopes, to our temptations and our trials; you will never be satiated in contemplating the manifold blessings which have been produced by the Holy Scriptures in human hearts, and in human households, and in cities, kingdoms, and nations, wherever the Scriptures have been duly received, loved, and obeyed.

Thus you will be confirmed, settled, and immoveably established in your belief, which Christ, speaking in His Church, solemnly testifies to be true, that *all*

---

² Ps. cxix. 162.   ³ Ps. cxix. 24. 97.
⁴ Ps. xix. 10.

Scripture is given by Inspiration of God[5]. And you may humbly believe and devoutly hope, that, if you have profited aright by its Revelations upon earth, it will be your employment and joy, in a future, eternal, state of existence, to have a fuller insight into those Mysteries, of which the Scriptures speak, and which *Angels desire to look into*[6]; and to have an everlasting vision in heaven, of the manifold wisdom of God.

[5] 2 Tim. iii. 16.   [6] 1 Pet. i. 12.

LECTURE V.

2 Timothy iii. 16, 17.

All Scripture is given by inspiration of God, and is profitable for doctrine, for reproof, for correction, for instruction in righteousness: that the man of God may be perfect, throughly furnished unto all good works.

I. *Be ready always to give an answer to every man that asketh you a reason of the hope that is in you.* This is the precept of St. Peter [1]. The hope that is in us, is grounded on a belief that the Bible is the Word of God; and the Apostle may therefore be understood to require us to be ready always to render to others an account of the reasons which constrain us, and ought to persuade them, to receive the Bible as God's Holy Word.

1. This being the case, we have in a previous discourse [2] declared ourselves unable to agree with those, who rest their belief in the Inspiration of the Bible on their own personal assurance of its Inspiration. Such an assurance, however satisfactory to them-

---

[1] 1 Pet. iii. 15.   [2] See above, pp. 20—27.

selves, can have no influence with other men; it will never bring the unbeliever to acknowledge the Bible to be from God.

2. Besides, the history of the last three centuries, and especially of our own age, has displayed the disastrous consequences of such a method of dealing with this great question of Inspiration.

The appeal to private feelings and assurances was first employed in *defence* of the Bible; but it has now been turned *against* it; and they who rely on private feelings and personal assurances, as their ground for *believing* the Bible, cannot make any effectual reply to those who appeal to their own private feelings and personal assurances as their reason for *rejecting* it.

The dogmas of Private Judgment have produced the doubts of Infidelity. The advantages which have been given to Scepticism by that appeal to personal feelings and private opinions, and the baneful fruits which it is now bringing forth in our own land, warn us to consider well our first principles.

3. We need something much more sound, solid, and stable, than our own consciousness, to refute the assaults of Unbelief, and to sustain our own faith and that of others in the divine Inspiration of the Bible; and also, if God so will, to bring the sceptic and unbeliever to acknowledge, that *all Scripture is given by Inspiration of God*.

4. It has been my endeavour to do something, with God's help, in this great work *of building up*

*our old waste places, and raising up the foundations of many generations*³ and *repairing the breach* that has been made by some, who ought themselves to be builders; and with this aim and purpose, the Discourses have been delivered on this subject which have been lately addressed to you in this place.

Reasonable men require sound reasons for what they do; and their assent to any proposition is proportioned to the reasons given in support of it; and the influence, which any proposition exercises on their conduct, is also proportioned to the conviction produced by those reasons in their minds.

II. What, then, are our *reasons* for belief in the Inspiration of Holy Scripture?

1. Our answer to this question, as you may remember, was: We have the authority of God Himself, declared to us in the uniform consent and practice of His own People, acknowledging the Old Testament to be His Word. We have that acknowledgment authorized and confirmed by the Son of God, when He came down from heaven and dwelt among us. And for our belief in the Inspiration of the New Testament as well as of the Old, we have Christ's testimony, speaking to us in the Church Universal, to which He has promised His presence and Spirit even to the end.

2. The peculiar value of this testimony to the Inspiration of Holy Scripture is its comprehensiveness and universality. *Other* arguments apply with

³ Isa. lviii. 12.

greater or less force to *portions* of Holy Writ. But *this* testimony extends to the *whole Bible.* It covers the whole with a divine panoply. It authenticates the whole as the Inspired Word of God; it proves, that *all Scripture—every part of Scripture—is given by Inspiration of God.*

III. To this point in the argument we had arrived in the last discourse.

Let us now proceed to observe, that the strength of this general testimony to the Inspiration of Holy Scripture is corroborated by other subsequent considerations, which accrue with cumulative force, and settle and stablish us more firmly in the belief, that the Scriptures are the Word of God.

IV. What, then, are these considerations?

This will be the subject of our present inquiry.

1. First, then, we are confirmed in our belief of the Inspiration of the Bible by observing the evidences of a *providential design* carried on during many ages in succession, for *protecting* the Bible, and for *assuring* us that Holy *Scripture is God's Word.*

If the Bible were *not* His Word, it would be nothing else than a *forgery* put forth in His name. For, it professes to deliver a message from God, and to give revelations of His nature and attributes, and to unfold the hidden mysteries of the spiritual world.

If, therefore, the Bible is *not* from God, it is a counterfeit coin, bearing His impress: it is a profane outrage against Him, and a fraudulent imposture upon mankind. Consequently it would be viewed

is confirmed by the evidence of God's providential care of the Bible.

with indignation by Him Who is a God of justice and truth.

But look back upon the past. Ever since the Bible was written, Almighty God has continued to *protect* it. He has never ceased to acknowledge it as His own. When the first books of the Bible—namely, the Books of Moses—were written, He received them under His divine guardianship in the Holy of Holies [4]. In critical times, He has ever interfered to save it. When the Old Testament was in peril of being lost, through the corruption and idolatry of Princes, Priests, and People, He brought forth the original volume of the Law from its sacred retreat in the days of good King Josiah, who in his own name, and in that of his people, proclaimed it to be the Word of God [5].

The subsequent dispersion of the Jews for their sins was made ministerial, as we have seen [6], to the preservation and dissemination of God's Holy Word in almost all countries, where Synagogues were erected by the Jews, in which the Old Testament was publicly read every Sabbath day.

Afterwards, in an evil time, Antiochus Epiphanes the King of Syria arose, and set up the abomination of desolation in the Temple of God at Jerusalem; and endeavoured to compel the Jews to worship the gods of the Heathen; and sent forth his own soldiers to destroy the copies of the Old Testament, who *rent*

---

[4] See above, p. 44.   [5] See above, p. 45.
[6] See above, pp. 35—39.

in pieces the Books of the Law which they found, and burnt them with fire; and whosoever was found with any such Book *was put to death* by the king's command [7].

In that critical juncture Almighty God interposed to rescue His own Word, and the persecuting King was suddenly cut off by a miserable death [8].

About a century and a half passed away, and the Son of God came down from heaven. At that time the Word of God was publicly read by the Jews in the Synagogues of Palestine, and in almost every city of the civilized world. But its sense was overlaid and obscured by human traditions. The Son of God acknowledged the Old Testament in the hands of the Jews. He owned it to be God's Word. He showed His zeal for it by sternly rebuking the Pharisees for making it of *none effect by their tradition* [9]. But He never rebuked them for receiving it as God's Word. No: on the contrary, He joined with them in the service of their Synagogues, and in reading and expounding the Old Testament as God's Word [1]. And His Apostles, and His Church after them, being taught by the Son of God, received the Old Testament as inspired by God; and commanded all men to receive it as such.

At the beginning of the fourth century after Christ, a fierce persecution arose against His Church. The Emperor of the Roman World, Diocletian, endea-

---

[7] 1 Mac. i. 54, 55—57.
[8] 1 Mac. vi. 12, 13. 16.   2 Mac. ix. 11—18. 28.
[9] Matt. xv. 3. 6.   [1] See above, pp. 60—65.

voured to destroy the Bible. He ordered diligent search to be made in all parts of the Empire for copies of the New Testament[2], and commanded them to be burnt. But God again interfered to save it. The sacred Bush *was burning, but it was not consumed,* and God's voice came forth from the midst of it[3]. In a few years afterwards, He raised up another Sovereign of the Roman World, Constantine, the first Emperor who embraced Christianity; and by his royal command copies of the Holy Scriptures were multiplied, and Churches were built, in which those Scriptures were read, as the inspired Word of God.

A thousand years passed away. Then was an evil time for Holy Scripture. The Bible was not dead; but it was buried. It was entombed in the sepulchre of a dead language. Not to speak of other lands, but only of our own, not a single copy of the Bible existed at that time in England in our tongue. But then arose John Wickliffe. Five hundred years ago, he translated the Bible into English[4]. In that age copies of the Bible could only be had in *manuscript;* and four and twenty years after his death it was decreed[5] by some in high place among us, that "no one should hereafter translate any text into English, and that no book of this kind should be read that was composed by John Wickliffe."

---

[2] Euseb. H. E. viii. 2.   [3] Exod. iii. 2. 4.
[4] See Lewis, History of the English Translations of the Bible, p. 18—27. Lond. 1739.
[5] By Archbishop Arundel, in a Constitution at Oxford, 1408.

Such was then the *famine of hearing God's Word*[6] in England.

But in fifty years' time, the art of Printing was invented, and William Caxton set up his press at Westminster[7]. And about the year 1526 William Tyndal made and published in London his Translation of the Bible—the *first* Translation that ever was *printed* in this land. The Author of this Translation, and his coadjutor John Frith, died nobly as Martyrs for the Faith; and the light which they kindled has never been put out. Two centuries and a half *after* the *first* Translation of the Bible into English by Wickliffe, and just two centuries and a half ago,—that is, in the year of our Lord 1611,—our own Authorized Version was published. That noble Translation was made by a goodly company of pious and learned men, at the head of whom stood a Dean of Westminster[8]; and by God's blessing on their labours, and on those of others in this and other lands, especially our religious Societies, the Holy Scriptures are now diffused every where. *Their sound is gone out into all lands, and their words into the ends of the world*[9]. *This is the Lord's doing, and it is marvellous in our eyes*[1].

Surely these events, extending over a range of more than three thousand years, afford practical attestation from God Himself, that the Bible is His

---

[6] Amos viii. 11. [7] A.D. 1474.
[8] Dean—afterwards Bishop—Andrewes. See Lewis's History of the Translations of the Bible, p. 308.
[9] Ps. xix. 4. [1] Ps. cxviii. 23.

Word. Surely they may inspire us with the cheering assurance, that, however Satan may assail it, God will protect it unto the end.

2. Another evidence of the Inspiration of Holy Scripture is seen in *the fulfilment of the Prophecies,* which are contained therein. God, and God alone, can foresee the future. He challenges false gods by saying, " *Show us what shall happen, declare us things for to come* [2]."

Let this test be applied to the Books of the Old Testament.

Can any other writings in the world be named, composed at such different times, in such different places, and by the instrumentality of such different persons, as the Books of the Old Testament; and delivering such a long series of Prophecies, as those, for instance, which concern the Messiah, and begin with the Book of Genesis, and end with that of Malachi; can any other writings be named, containing Prophecies so minute, so various, and *seemingly* so contradictory—as, for example, those which pre-announce a Messiah, suffering the most shameful and agonizing pain, and yet triumphing as a mighty Conqueror, and reigning as a glorious King—and all punctually fulfilled, fulfilled by the agency of that very people—the Jews—who had those prophecies in their hands, and who read those prophecies *every Sabbath Day* in their Synagogues; and yet, as St.

[2] Isa. xli. 22.

Paul says, *fulfilled them in condemning Him*, of whom those Prophecies speak?

Here, then, is another proof that the Books of the Old Testament are animated by the breath of God.

3. Consider also the wonderful *symmetry of the various parts of the Bible*.

Its subject-matter reaches from the Creation to the End of time. Its Books were written by different persons in distant ages and countries. And yet how marvellously do they harmonize together. They are like Christ's *vesture, woven without seam* [3]. They are like the wings of the Cherubim, as described by Ezekiel, intertwined and interlaced together [4]. The Jewish Doctors said that the words of the Pentateuch make *one word;* and there is a spiritual truth in the saying. The Books of the Bible are all fitted together. The Law prepares the way for the Prophets, and the Prophets proclaim the sanctity of the Law. The New Testament lies hid in the Old Testament, and the Old Testament is opened in the New. All the Books of the Bible are joined together, and form *one Book*.

No human design could have produced such a result as this. It is the work of Him who sees all things at a glance *to the end from the beginning* [5], and with Whom *one day is as a thousand years, and a thousand years as one day* [6].

Here is another evidence that the Bible is from Him.

[3] John xix. 23.
[4] Ezek. i. 9. 11, 12.
[5] Isa. xlvi. 10.
[6] 2 Pet. iii. 8.

4. Let us also reflect *what kind of persons* they were, who were *employed* to *write* the Bible.

The Bible, particularly the New Testament, professes to unfold things *hidden from the foundation of the world*[7]. The Gospels claim to be records of the sayings of the Son of God, revealing the abstruse Mysteries of His heavenly Kingdom. And *who* were the persons *chosen* to write these marvels? Their enemies justly said that they were *unlearned and ignorant men*[8]. True: such they were in *themselves*, Publicans and Fishermen of Galilee. Yet these *unlearned and ignorant* men have become the Teachers of the World. They are the Historians of the greatest deeds that ever were done; they are the Chroniclers of the wisest sayings that were ever uttered; they are the reporters of the most heavenly Sermons that were ever preached. And the World has received their words,—has received them as divine. The Gospels are read every where. God evangelized the learned and wise by means of the simple and foolish; and not the simple and foolish by means of the learned and wise. As S. Augustine says, "He caught the Orator by the Fisherman[9]; and not the Fisherman by the Orator."

The greatest sages of this world—the Bacons and Newtons, the Keplers and Pascals—sit down as

---

[7] Matt. xiii. 35. [8] Acts iv. 13.
[9] Piscatorem de Oratore non lucratus est Christus, sed Oratorem de Piscatore. S. Augustine, de Utilitate Jejunii ix., and Serm. xliii. and lxxxvii., and in Ps. cxlix.

little children at the feet of St. Matthew and St. John.

How could this be done?

Certainly not by the writers themselves. *Of themselves they could do nothing. Their sufficiency was of God*[1]. According to His promise, Christ sent them the Holy Ghost, *to lead them into all truth, and to bring all things to their remembrance, whatsoever He had said to them.*

He *chose weak instruments* for this *mighty work* of evangelizing the world, in order that by the *weakness of the instruments chosen*, and by the *greatness of the work done* through their instrumentality, it might be evident to all, that the work was not of them, but of God. The treasure of heavenly truth was committed to earthen vessels, in order that the *excellency of the power of the Gospel* might be seen *to be of God, and not of men*[2].

5. Let us reflect also on the beneficent *effects produced* by *the Bible* on the world.

Here is another proof that the Scriptures are from Him. The Bible speaks in God's name, and professes to be God's Word. And *if* it is not in fact, what in name it professes to be, then there is no other alternative, it is not from God, but from the Evil One. *Every plant which My Heavenly Father hath not planted, shall be rooted up,* says Christ[3]. And, *A Tree is known by its fruits*[4].

---

[1] 2 Cor. iii. 5. [2] 2 Cor. iv. 7.
[3] Matt. xv. 13. [4] Matt. vii. 16; xii. 33. Luke vi. 43.

What, then, have been the *fruits* of the Bible?

Do they not show that the tree is a good tree, that it is a tree of life, and *that its leaves are for the healing of the Nations* [5].

This is the fact on which St. Paul insists, when he says that *All Scripture*, or rather *every Scripture* [6], *being divinely inspired*, or *inbreathed by God, is also* [7] *profitable for doctrine, for reproof, for correction, for instruction in righteousness, that the man of God may be perfect, throughly furnished unto every good work.* What is the condition of men without it? and what is their condition, wherever they receive and obey it?

The Bible, and the Bible alone, makes subjects loyal to their Sovereigns, because it teaches them that, in obeying their Sovereign, they are obeying God, and will be rewarded hereafter by Him [8]. The Bible, and the Bible alone, makes Sovereigns rule rightly, because it reminds them that they must render a strict account of their rule to the King of kings. The Bible makes Judges and Magistrates judge just judgment, because it tells them, that they must one day stand before the Judgment-Seat of Christ. The Bible makes Masters kind to their Servants, because it declares to all Masters, that they have *a Master in heaven* [1]. The Bible makes Servants faithful to their Masters, because it assures all Ser-

---

[5] Rev. xxii. 2.

[6] πᾶσα γραφή: "Every portion of the Holy Book is inspired, and forms a living portion of a living organic whole."

[7] καί; this is probably the true reading of the text.

[8] Rom. xiii. 1—3.   [1] Eph. vi. 9. Col. iv. 1.

vants that they are Christ's *freemen*, and will receive a reward for dutiful service, at the Great Day [2]. The Bible persuades busy men to forego their business, and makes tender women forget their tenderness, and visit Prisons and Hospitals, and minister at the bedside of the sick, and watch over the dying; because they know, that what they do to *the least of Christ's brethren* on earth, they do *it unto Him*, and that He will requite them for it at the Great Day [3]. The Bible, and the Bible alone, unlocks the fetters of the slave, and makes all men *brethren in Christ* [4]. The Bible sends forth the Missionary to heathen lands, to loose the chains of the soul. The Bible, and the Bible alone, operates on the mainspring of human actions,—*the heart*. The Bible makes men honest and just, kind and charitable in their *thoughts* and *speeches*, as well as in their *acts*, because it teaches them, that *all things are naked and open to the eyes of Him with Whom they have to do* [5], and that He will bring *to light the hidden things of darkness, and make manifest the counsels of the hearts* [6]. The Bible makes Husbands and Wives faithful and loving to each other, because it teaches, that Marriage was instituted by God in Paradise, and that it represents the spiritual union and wedlock between Christ and His Church, and that whoever dishonours Marriage desecrates a great Mystery [7]. The Bible makes young men and

[2] Eph. vi. 5. Col. iii. 22. Titus ii. 9. 1 Pet. ii. 18. 22.
[3] Matt. xxv. 40. [4] Phil. 16.
[5] Heb. iv. 13. [6] 1 Cor. iv. 5.
[7] Eph. v. 22—32.

young women to live pure, chaste, and holy lives, because it teaches them that *their bodies are temples of the Holy Ghost*, and that whosoever *defiles the Temple of God, him will God destroy*[8], and that *their bodies are members of Christ*, and are to be held *in honour as such*[9]; and that their bodies will be raised again from the grave, and that they must then give an account of the *things done in the body*[1], and that, if they have presented their bodies a *living sacrifice* to God upon earth[2], in holiness and pureness of living, their bodies will rise from the grave, and live hereafter in heaven, in everlasting health and angelic beauty, and *be made like unto Christ's glorious body, according to the mighty working whereby He is able to subdue all things unto Himself*[3].

What shall we say more? The Bible is the fountain of all true Patriotism and Loyalty in States; it is the source of all true wisdom, sound policy, and equity in Senates, Council-chambers, and Courts of Justice; it is the spring of all true discipline and obedience, and of all valour and chivalry in Armies and Fleets, on the battle-field, and on the wide sea. It is the origin of all probity and integrity in Commerce and in Trade, in Marts and in Shops, in Banking-houses and Exchanges; in the public resorts of men, and in the secret silence of the heart. It is the pure unsullied fountain of all love and peace, happiness,

---

[8] 1 Cor. iii. 16, 17; vi. 19.   [9] 1 Cor. vi. 15.   1 Thess. iv. 4.
[1] Rom. ii. 6; xiv. 12.   2 Cor. v. 10.   [2] Rom. xii. 1.
[3] Phil. iii. 21.

quietness, and joy, in families and households. Wherever it is duly obeyed, it makes the *desert* of the World *to rejoice and blossom as the rose*[4].

These are the fruits of the Bible. Surely we may conclude from them, that the Tree which bears them has been planted by the hand of God, and is watered by the dews and showers of His Spirit, and is warmed by the sunshine of His grace;—that it is God's Tree, and will flourish for evermore.

V. Finally, let us look around. The place in which we now are, is full of instruction. In this ancient Minster, Kings and Queens are crowned: and at their Coronation, that Sacred Volume, the HOLY BIBLE, is taken from that Altar; and that Blessed Book is placed in the Monarch's hands, with these solemn words, uttered by the public Voice of the English Church and Nation, at that august ceremonial[5]:—

"Our Gracious Sovereign! we present you with this Book, the most valuable thing that this world affords. Here is Wisdom; this is the Royal Law; these are the lively Oracles of God. Blessed is he that readeth, and they that keep the Words of this Book; that keep and do the things contained in it. For these are the words of eternal Life, able to make you wise and happy in this world, nay, wise unto salvation; and so, happy for evermore, through faith

[4] Isa. xxxv. 1.
[5] See the Form and Order of Coronation of the Kings and Queens of Great Britain and Ireland, in the Abbey Church of St. Peter, Westminster.

which is in Christ Jesus; to whom be glory for ever. Amen."

Again look around. We are assembled here to-day on the eve of a funeral—the funeral of the venerated Mother of our beloved Queen. Meditations on royal deaths, and on royal funerals, find a proper place here. For here Kings and Queens rest in their graves. Here Princes and Nobles sleep in the dust. Here lie Statesmen and Orators, Legislators and Judges, Philosophers, Poets, and Historians, Captains and Conquerors.

Now consider this.

At their last hour, when the shadows of death were falling upon them, when the heart was beating feebly and faintly, and the hand could hardly prop the drooping head, when the eyes were beginning to be bedimmed with the cloud and mist of mortality, where, then, was their stay and support? At that awful hour, did the Sovereign find any solid comfort in meditating on the vast extent of his dominions, or on the long duration of his reign? Did the Princes and Nobles, who here lie buried, derive any genuine consolation from the splendour of their stately mansions, or the beauty of their wide demesnes, or from their patrician badges and titles, and the long line of their ancestral dignities? No: at that solemn hour, all these were vanishing like a dream. Did the Statesman obtain any comfortable assurance from his political sagacity, or the Orator from his brilliant eloquence? No: these things were like fading flowers. Did the Legislator or the Judge find any assistance in their Codes and Law Books? No: they themselves were summoned to Judgment. Could the Philosopher solace himself with musing on his Problems and Theories, or the Poet with the remembrance of his songs? No: these *were like a tale that is told*[6]. Could the Historian procure peace for his soul from his records of past ages? No: he himself was passing away. Could the seafaring Captain obtain a spiritual calm from his long voyages to distant climes? No: he must now take another voyage to an unexplored region, where no earthly chart or compass would guide him. He must now set sail for Eternity. Did the General or Admiral,—the heroes of many battles,—gather hope and joy for themselves from their laurels gained in the conflicts of war? No: they must prepare now for a sharper struggle with Spiritual Powers, against which the Artillery of this World would be of no avail. But, had they, then, *no* comfort in that hour of Death? Miserable, miserable indeed, if such was then the case. Had they no comfort? And if they had, where was it? It was in the Bible. If they had believed its doctrines, and had obeyed its precepts, and if they had trusted in its promises, if they had lived and fed on it as living bread from heaven, then there was hope in their end. Then there was peace in their death, through the might and mercy of Him who died for them, and was buried, and over-

[6] Ps. xc. 9.

came, and rose again, and opened the kingdom of heaven to all believers. Then, though *they walked through the valley and shadow of death, they feared no evil, for He was with them*[7]. Then they fell asleep in peace, and in hope to awake with joy. Then Death to them was Birth,—Birth to endless life. Then they felt, in their inmost hearts, that belief in the Inspiration of the Bible—a belief based on the soundest reason—is able to speak comfort to the soul. Then they realized its power. Then it proved its virtue. Then they knew that *whatsoever had been written aforetime had been written for their learning, that they through patience and comfort of the Scriptures might have hope*[8]. Then they found, by personal experience, that a few verses of the Bible, heard with the ear of faith, are of more worth than crowns and coronets; that they are of more value than all the wealth and grandeur, all the mansions and estates, all the eloquence and wisdom, all the genius and science, all the triumphs and trophies, of this world. Then they drank a refreshing stream of heavenly peace and joy from such blessed words as these, *I am the Resurrection, and the life*, saith the Lord: *he that believeth in Me, though he were dead, yet shall he live: and he that liveth and believeth in Me shall never die*[9]. *Verily, verily, I say unto you, He that heareth My word, and believeth on Him that sent Me, hath everlasting life, and shall not come into condemnation, but is passed from death unto*

[7] Ps. xxiii. 4.   [8] Rom. xv. 4.   [9] John xi. 25, 26.

life[1]. Then they were able to say, *O Death, where is thy sting? O Grave, where is thy Victory? Thanks be to God who giveth us the Victory through our Lord Jesus Christ*[2]. Then there was divine music for them in those heavenly words, *I heard a voice from heaven, saying unto me, Write, Blessed are the dead which die in the Lord: even so, saith the Spirit, for they rest from their labours*[3].

Brethren, may this support be yours, in your last hour! It *will be* yours, be sure, if you live and die in the belief, that *all Scripture is given by inspiration of God.* And hereafter, at the great and dreadful Day, when the *Elements shall melt with fervent heat*[4], and when the Volume of this visible Creation will no more be legible; when all the fair characters now written in earth and sky upon the pages of the Book of Nature, will be effaced and obliterated, and the heavens themselves *will depart as a scroll*[5],—then the Word of God will remain unchanged; its letters will be indelible, they will *endure for ever*[6]. *Heaven and earth shall pass away*, says Christ, *but My Words shall not pass away*[7]. Blessed, therefore, is he that heareth and keepeth *the sayings of that Book*[8], blessed indeed is he—blessed for evermore!

[1] John v. 24.
[2] 1 Cor. xv. 55.
[3] Rev. xiv. 13.
[4] 2 Pet. iii. 10.
[5] Isa. xxxiv. 4. Rev. vi. 14.
[6] 1 Pet. i. 25.
[7] Matt. xxiv. 35.
[8] Rev. i. 3; xxii. 7.

THE END.

GILBERT AND RIVINGTON, PRINTERS, ST. JOHN'S SQUARE, LONDON.

LATELY PUBLISHED,

BY THE AUTHOR OF THIS VOLUME.

THE GREEK TESTAMENT,

With Introductions and Notes.

I. THE FOUR GOSPELS. *New Edition.* 1*l.* 1*s.*
II. THE ACTS OF THE APOSTLES. *New Edition.* 10*s.* 6*d.*
III. ST. PAUL'S EPISTLES. 1*l.* 11*s.* 6*d.*
IV. THE GENERAL EPISTLES, AND THE BOOK OF REVELATION. 1*l.* 1*s.*

Any of the above Parts may be had separately.

An INDEX to the whole work, by the Rev. JOHN TWYCROSS, of the Charterhouse, price 4*s.*; allowed to purchasers of all the parts of the Edition.

The GREEK TEXT of ST. PAUL'S EPISTLES, arranged in *Chronological order*, may be had in the same size and type as the above, price 5*s.* 6*d.*

RIVINGTONS, WATERLOO PLACE, PALL MALL.

www.ingramcontent.com/pod-product-compliance
Lightning Source LLC
Chambersburg PA
CBHW021941160426
43195CB00011B/1181